THE MET | DK

5OOO
YEARS OF
AWESOME OBJECTS →

A HISTORY OF ART **FOR CHILDREN**

THE MET | DK

5000 YEARS OF AWESOME OBJECTS →

A HISTORY OF ART FOR CHILDREN

SUSIE BROOKS, SUSIE HODGE, DR. SARAH RICHTER,
MARY RICHARDS, AND DR. AARON ROSEN

CONTENTS

Marble Statue of a Lion
Greek, ca. 400–390 BCE

INTRODUCTION 8

ANCIENT ART
12

The First Artists 14

MATERIALS
Stone 16
Animal Materials 18
Wood 20
Metal 22
Clay 24
Paint 26
Cloth 28
Paper 30

ANCIENT NEAR EAST
Ancient Mesopotamia 32
Great Cities 34
Early Writing 36
Agriculture and Animal Symbolism 37
Art Making 38
Storytelling 40

ANCIENT EGYPT 42
Life on the Nile 44
God and Goddesses 46

Making Art 48
Architecture 50
Art for the Afterlife 52

ANCIENT GREECE 54
Making Art 56
Storytelling 58

ANCIENT ROME 60
Making Art 62
Roman Homes 64
Religious Beliefs 66

ARMS AND ARMOR
Don't lose your head! 68
Armor for the Body 70
Weapons and Shields 72

ASIAN ART
Animals in Asian Art 74
Jade in China 76
Ceremonies and Rituals in China 78
The Beginnings of Buddhist Art 80
Buddhism Across Asia 82

THE AMERICAS
Central America, South America, and Mexico 84
The Sculpture of Mesoamerica 86
Making Art 88
Cities 90

THE MEDIEVAL PERIOD

92

Camelid Figurine
Inca, 1400–1533

ISLAMIC ART 94

A Place to Pray 96

The Art of Words 98

The Art of Science 100

Tiles 102

THE BYZANTINE EMPIRE 104

Icons 106

Mighty Mosaics 108

Byzantine Luxury 110

MUSICAL INSTRUMENTS

Percussion 112

Wind Instruments 114

Stringed Instruments 116

ASIAN ART

Trade 118

Silk and Paper 120

Protective Deities and Guardians 122

Buddhism in the Himalayas 124

Porcelain 126

EUROPE

Medieval Europe 128

Stained Glass Windows 130

Illuminated Manuscripts 132

Medieval Tapestries 134

Pouring and Storing 136

Playing Cards 138

Censer in the Form of a Mythical Beast
China, early 17th century

APPROACHING THE MODERN ERA
140

Ceramic Horn
France, late 18th or early 19th century

ASIAN ART
Landscapes of East Asia 142
Lacquer 144
The Great Wave 146
Japanese Fashion and Style 148
Zodiac Figures 150

ISLAMIC ART
Timurid Empire 152
Mughal Dynasty 154
Safavid Dynasty 156
The Ottoman Empire 158

THE AMERICAS
The Aztecs 160
The Inca 162

EUROPE
Gold Paintings in Italy 164
New Subjects 166
Spanish Painting 168
Flanders 170
Woodcuts and Printing 172
Britain 174
France 176
Catching a Scene 178
   Vessels 180

AFRICAN ART
Portraits of Kingship 182
Ere Ibeji Twin Figures 184
Seeing Privacy 186
Sacred Stools 188
Tracking History 190

OCEANIA 192

NORTH AMERICA
American Life 194
American Scenes 196
   Furniture 198
   Fashion 202
   Undergarments and Accessories 204
   Adornment 206

THE MODERN ERA
208

LATE 19TH CENTURY

Nature.. 210

Cities... 212

Leisure 214

Self-Portraits 216

EARLY 20TH CENTURY

Form 218

Color.. 220

Time... 222

Bold Abstractions............................ 224

MID 20TH CENTURY

Surrealism.. 226

Finding Form 228

Everyday Life 230

Chairs.. 232

LATE 20TH CENTURY

New Experiments................................ 234

Art and Activism 236

LATE 20TH AND EARLY 21ST CENTURY

History and Memory.............................. 238

21ST CENTURY

Digital Art.. 240

Climate Change................................... 242

QUIZ!

Test Your Knowledge 244

Index.. 248

Answers to Quiz 254

Picture Credits 255

Acknowledgments............................... 256

The Little Fourteen-Year-Old Dancer

Edgar Degas (French), 1880–1881, cast by A. A. Hébrard, 1922, tutu 2018

INTRODUCTION

5OOO YEARS OF AWESOME OBJECTS →

A HISTORY OF ART FOR CHILDREN

Welcome to 5,000 years of art! In this book, you'll discover objects from all across the world, of all shapes and sizes, from a tiny Japanese fish hook to a vast Egyptian temple. The objects you'll see in these pages are from the collection of one of the largest museums in the world, The Metropolitan Museum of Art in New York City, in the United States, and are often on display there. Behind the scenes at the Museum, people work to look after the objects, studying their history and taking care to protect them so they can be enjoyed for years to come.

The book is organized in chronological order and explores art made by different people in different places within each time period.

Section 1, Ancient Art, contains hundreds of unique objects made by the artists of the ancient world. We begin with a series of themed pages (pages 14–31), which explore materials used across many regions and cultures: stone, animal materials, wood, metal, clay, paint, cloth, and paper. Pages 32–91 look at particular regions in more detail and are filled with objects that have remained safe for thousands of years, deeply buried in tombs, wrapped in layers of cloth in sealed boxes and chambers, or preserved in the ground beneath layers of stone and earth.

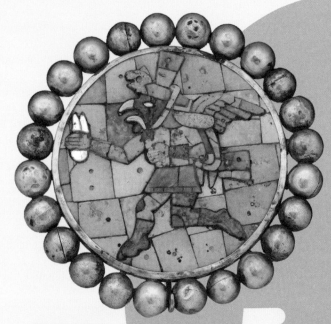

Ear Ornament, Winged Runner
Moche, 400–700 CE

Feline Bottle
Tembladera, Peru, 600–400 BCE

Medallion with the Virgin from an Icon Frame

Byzantine, ca. 1100

In Section 2, The Medieval Period, we look first at the precious objects and books filled with sacred calligraphy made in the Islamic world, then at the mighty mosaics, holy figures, and luxurious jeweled objects of the Byzantine Empire. Our journey continues with the painted scrolls, glazed ceramics, exquisite lacquerware, and fine textiles produced in Asia during the Middle Ages and the illuminated manuscripts and detailed tapestries made in Medieval Europe.

With Section 3, Approaching the Modern Era, we look in detail at innovations that sprang up in many regions across the world from around 1300. We see Italian paintings created with gold leaf; royal sculpture crafted in bronze in West Africa; the textiles of the Aztecs and Inca in Mesoamerica; the landscape paintings of East Asia and woodblock prints of Japan; the finely detailed paintings of the Mughal Empire; and the landscape paintings of France, Britain, and the United States.

The Spy Zambur Brings Mahiya to the City of Tawariq
Attributed to Mah Muhammad and Kesav Das (Indian), ca. 1570

Standing Figure with Feathered Headdress
Iran, 12th–early 13th century

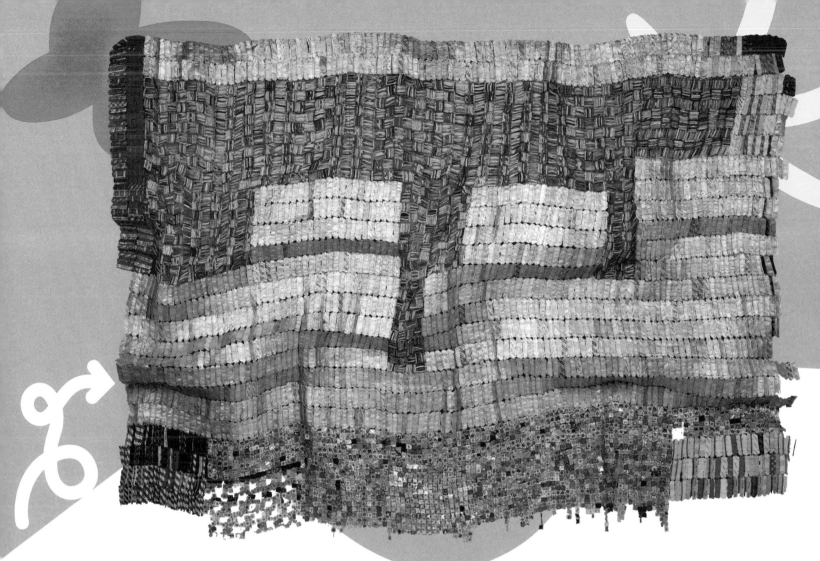

Between Earth and Heaven
El Anatsui (Ghanaian), 2006

Section 4, The Modern Age, explores the objects, paintings, and sculptures of the past 200 years. From early photography to sculptures and installations from the last ten years, we explore—in a series of pages arranged by theme—the way our changing world affects the way artists work and the materials they use.

Scattered through these eras, you will find special sections on particular objects through time, such as Arms and Armor (pages 68–73), Musical Instruments (pages 112–117), Vessels (pages 180–181), Furniture (pages 196–199), and Fashion (pages 202–205). These allow you to directly compare finely crafted objects from different times and places.

One of the best ways to learn about a society is by looking at the objects it makes. Objects can tell us about beliefs, culture, science, entertainment, and the rituals of daily life. As well as setting out some differences, the objects we make also show us what we have in common with people who lived even as long as 5,000 years ago.

1.
ANCIENT ART

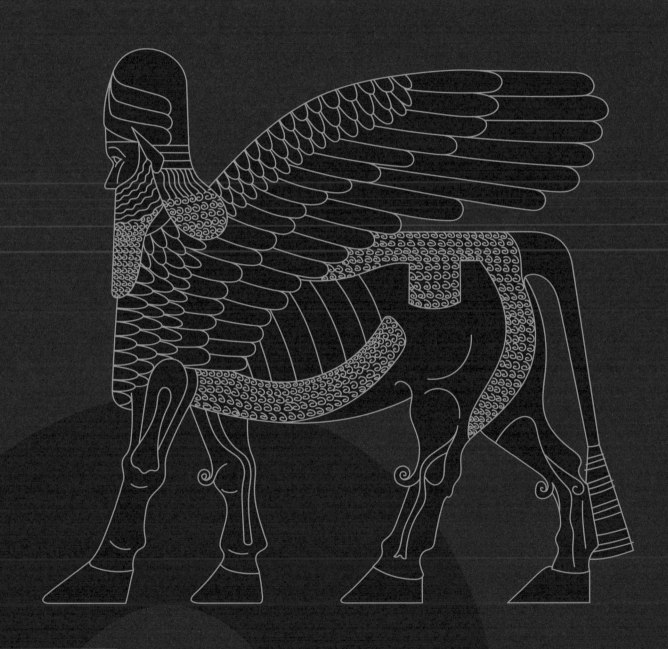

THE FIRST ARTISTS

Early stone tools would have initally been used for hunting prey, cutting hides, carving meat, and chopping plants for food. Later, they were used to make marks that we would call art. Red ocher tablets with motifs scratched into them have been discovered in Blombos Cave in South Africa. They are from 73,000 years ago and are believed to be among the earliest examples of ideas and information recorded through pictures. 75,000-year-old palettes filled with pigments used to paint stone surfaces were also found at the same site, as well as evidence of a bead-making industry. Paintings were being created on cave walls as early as 40,000 years ago—in places as far apart in place and time as Chauvet Cave in France and Cave of the Hands in Argentina.

Did you know?

The first tools may have been made as long as 3 million years ago. They were made by our very distant ancestors. Modern humans emerged around 250,000 years ago, probably in what is now known as east Africa.

Nine Hand Axes
discovered in Aisne, France,
700,000–200,000 BCE
Flint and quartzite

These hand axes, known as bifaces, were created by fashioning flint into symmetrical tear-shaped objects. Some were suitable for a variety of tasks, including digging, scraping, and chopping. Some were prized for their appearance rather than functionality. Tools like these were made by many species of our ancient human relatives, over a period of 1.7 million years.

Hand Ax
Egypt, ca. 240,000–40,000 BCE
Flint

Our Neanderthal ancestors developed new ways of fashioning flint into hand tools. They developed a particular technique for shaping these tools, which archaeologists called Levallois after the French region where many tools were discovered.

Early Sculpture

Early artists also made small, portable objects from bone, ivory, antlers, clay, and stone. These often took the form of humans, like this female figure, or animals. We don't know exactly what these works were used for, but versions of them were made for thousands of years. Were they goddesses or good luck charms? Would they have been used in rituals or ceremonies? Perhaps they were passed down over generations, from parents to children.

White Cross-lined Ware Beaker with Nile River Scene
Egypt, ca. 3650–3500 BCE

Early Painting

This beaker, dating from around 3650–3500 BCE, is an example of early painting. It depicts a scene on the River Nile, with hippos painted on one side and crocodiles on the other.

Seated Female Figure
Iraq or Syria, ca. 5600–5000 BCE
Painted ceramic

STONE

Stone varies widely in composition, texture, and hardness, and often requires specialized skills to carve. Softer limestone was better suited for carving with inscriptions, like the Egyptian stela opposite, whereas diorite is a much harder stone. Different types of stone were abundant in different regions. Jade was used thousands of years ago by artisans in Asia and Mesoamerica—the green stone was found both in the Yangtze River Delta in China and in the Motagua River Valley in Guatemala. Marble, the preferred stone of ancient Greek and Roman sculptors, was abundant around the Mediterranean. Although stone is relatively durable, it can be damaged or broken by people and the environment. Ancient stone sculptures are often found broken into fragments, like these feet that were once joined to a body and the marble hand holding a scroll, pictured on the opposite page.

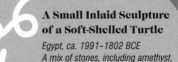
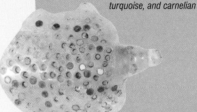

A Small Inlaid Sculpture of a Soft-Shelled Turtle
Egypt, ca. 1991–1802 BCE
A mix of stones, including amethyst, turquoise, and carnelian

Plaque with the Name of Amenhotep III Flanked by Two Snakes
Egypt, ca. 1390–1352 BCE
Carnelian

Colorful stone

Precious stones like deep-blue lapis lazuli, from northeast Afghanistan, were prized for their intense color. The stone was popular in the art of ancient Iraq and Syria; here, it has been used in an eye inlay (a piece added separately, often in a contrasting color) for a statue. Jade was prized for its color, too, which could be light green like the Mayan Pair of Earflare Frontals, or dark like the Ritual Object from China.

Water Buffalo
China, 13th–11th century BCE
Jade

Pair of Earflare Frontals
Maya, 3rd–6th century CE
Jade

Eye Inlay For a Statue
Iraq, ca. 2600–2500 BCE
Lapis lazuli, shell

Ritual Object
China, ca. 2400 BCE
Jade

Marble Calyx-Krater with Reliefs of Maidens and Dancing Maenads

Roman, 1st century CE
Marble

Marble Capital and Finial in the Form of a Sphinx

Greek, ca. 530 BCE
Marble

Stela of the Gatekeeper Maati

Egypt, ca. 2051–2030 BCE
Limestone

Limestone is a soft rock that is easy to carve. The carvings on this stela (a stone slab used for commemorative purposes) are still clearly visible.

Indra

India, ca. 2nd century
Sandstone

Head of Gudea

Iraq, ca. 2150–2100 BCE
Diorite

Marble Head of a Young Woman from a Funerary Statue

Greek, late 4th century BCE
Marble

Marble Female Figure

Cyclades,
3200–2800 BCE
Marble

Base and Feet of a Worshiper

Iraq, ca. 2500–2350 BCE
Alabaster

Marble Left Hand Holding a Scroll

Roman, 1st or 2nd century CE
Marble

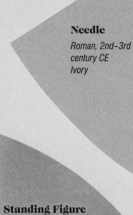

Needle

Roman, 2nd–3rd century CE
Ivory

Did you know?

Many of the ivory objects pictured here are made from elephant tusks. Tragically, in modern times, trade in ivory has led to the near extinction of elephants. Asian elephants once lived in ancient Syria but were hunted to extinction by the 8th century BCE, in part because of the demand for ivory. Trading ivory is now banned in most countries worldwide.

Standing Figure

Alaska, 2nd century BCE– 1st century CE
Ivory

A Tusk Figurine of a Man

Egypt, ca. 3900–3500 BCE
Ivory

Spoon with a Falcon on the Handle

Egypt, ca. 3300–3100 BCE
Ivory

Writing Palette and Brushes of Princess Meketaten

Egypt, ca. 1353–1336 BCE
Ivory, rush, red, yellow, and black pigments

Plaque with Cat Head

Iraq, ca. 9th–8th century BCE
Ivory

Game of Hounds and Jackals

Egypt, ca. 1814–1805 BCE
Ebony and ivory

Comb Decorated with a Hippo

Egypt, ca. 3900–3500 BCE
Ivory

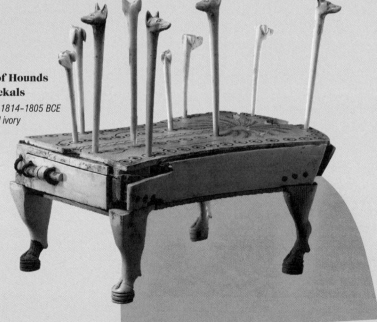

ANIMAL MATERIALS

Many of the materials used to make the earliest known artworks come from animals. All the objects shown here were made from the bones, teeth, tusks, shells, or horns of animals. Chemically, ivory and bone are quite similar, but physically, they are very different. *Ivory* is the name for the hard, dense materials that come from the teeth or tusks of animals like hippo, elephant, or walrus. Bone has a spongier texture. Shells and horn have a different chemical makeup; shell is chemically similar to limestone, and horn is similar to nails and hair.

Sometimes, artists used the natural shapes of bones, horns, antlers, and tusks to create objects—like the figurine of a man from Egypt, shown on the page opposite. Shells are already fashioned into beautiful shapes by nature and often have patterned or iridescent surfaces; the Egyptian mother-of-pearl shell, below, has been pierced with two holes so it can be worn around the neck. Look at the clam shell from the Eastern Mediterranean next to it; its natural shape has been sculpted into a female head.

Pair of Clappers
Egypt, ca. 1353–1336 BCE
Ivory

Arrowhead
Japan, ca. 1000–300 BCE
Bone

Beads
Iran, ca. 9th century BCE
Cowrie shells and stone

Fish Hook
Japan, ca. 1000–300 BCE
Bone

Fragment of a Tridacna (a Type of Clam) Shell with a Sculpted Female Head
Eastern Mediterranean, ca. 7th century BCE

Mother-of-Pearl Shell Inscribed with the Cartouche of Senwosret I
Egypt, ca. 1961–1917 BCE or later

WOOD

The wooden objects shown on these pages were expertly carved by artists who understood the natural properties of specific wood types, such as grain, texture, and hardness. Large wooden boards were used to carve reliefs like the example from India depicting the goddess Durga, shown on the left. Smaller pieces were fashioned into functional objects like the Peruvian snuff tray, on the opposite page. As carpenters do today, carpenters of long ago developed different ways of joining wood, including fitted joints, wooden dowels, and, later, nails. Wood takes paint well, so it can be decorated; look at the colors on the painted coffin of Khnumhotep from Egypt and at the shine on the lacquered ram from China. Wood can be bent to make a bow, like the bow harp, or constructed into a container, like the Egyptian game box, which has a drawer for storing game pieces! Over time, wood deteriorates due to a variety of reasons, including humidity and insect activity. Although some of these objects are well preserved, many show damage, like the crack you can see in the statue of Tjeteti.

Plaque with the Goddess Durga Standing on a Lotus
India, 1st century BCE

Bow Harp
Egypt, ca. 2030–1640 BCE

Statue of Tjeteti in Middle Age
Egypt, ca. 2200–2152 BCE

Traveling Boat Being Rowed
Egypt, ca. 1981–1975 BCE

Beaker (Kero)

*Bolivia or Peru,
7th–10th century*

**Writing Board of an
Apprentice Scribe**

Egypt, ca. 2030 BCE

Mirror-Bearer

Maya, 6th century

**Game Box
Inscribed for Taia
and His Family**

Egypt, ca. 1550–1295 BCE

Coffin of Khnumhotep

Egypt, ca. 1981–1802 BCE

Kneeling Ram

China, 206 BCE–220 CE

Hatnefer's Chair

Egypt, ca. 1492–1473 BCE

Snuff Tray

*Wari, Peru,
4th–10th century*

**Kohl Tube
and Stick**

Egypt, ca. 1550–1458 BCE

**Standing Female
Attendant**

*China, late 7th century–early
8th century*

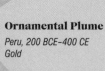

Ornamental Plume

Peru, 200 BCE–400 CE
Gold

Did you know?

Many metal objects from ancient times were melted down so that the metal could be repurposed. This makes the objects that survive today even more important.

Statuette of Amun

Egypt, ca. 945–712 BCE
Gold

Mirror with Hathor Emblem Handle

Egypt, ca. 1479–1425 BCE
Disk: silver; handle: wood (modern) sheathed in gold (ancient); the inlays are modern

Sandals

Egypt, ca. 1479–1425 BCE
Gold

Ax-Head with Bird-Headed Demon, Boar, and Dragon

Central Asia, ca. late 3rd–early 2nd millennium BCE
Silver, gold foil

Ritual Wine Container (*Yu*) with Lid

China, late 11th century BCE
Bronze

Lion's Head

Iran, ca. 9th century BCE
Bronze

Ax

China, 12th–11th century BCE
Bronze

Dōtaku (Bronze Bell)

China, 1st–2nd century

Foundation Peg in the Form of the Forepart of a Lion

Syria, ca. 2200–2100 BCE
Copper alloy

Large Brooch

European Bronze Age, 1100–1000 BCE
Copper alloy

Safety Pin

Italy, 10th century BCE
Bronze

METAL

Great innovations in metalworking presented artists with new ways of making objects. Some metals like gold occur naturally, but many other metals have to be transformed from their mineral form found in rocks by heating in a furnace—a process known as smelting. Metals can be hammered into shape or melted and cast using molds. The sandals on the opposite page and the vulture pectoral (a piece of armor worn on the chest) below were made from hammered gold sheets. The body of the Statuette of Amun, opposite, was cast from one piece of gold.

Mixing different metals together produces alloys, which have different properties to the individual metals. For instance, mixing copper and tin produces bronze, which can then be melted and poured into molds made of clay, sand, or other materials in a process called casting (to read more about bronze casting, see page 79).

Even though iron-containing minerals are abundant and easy to obtain, it took a long time for people to understand how they could be used. Given its high melting point, iron could not be melted easily in ancient times. Instead, it could be worked into tools and weapons by heating and hammering in a forge.

Vulture Pectoral
Egypt, ca. 1479–1425 BCE
Gold

Fish Hook
Egypt, ca. 1295–1070 BCE
Bronze

Did you know?

Early pots and vessels—like the cooking pot made in Japan in the Jomon period—were shaped and smoothed by hand. The potter built up the pot by coiling rings of clay on top of each other, layer by layer. But with the invention of the pottery wheel (which was at first a simple platform turned by hand), pots could be formed more quickly: now, potters could take a single piece of clay and spin it fast while shaping it with their fingers or other tools.

Cooking Pot

Japan, 10,500–3000 BCE
Earthenware

Mycenaean Female Figurines

Helladic Mycenaean, ca. 1400–1300 BCE
Terracotta

Jar (Hu)

China, ca. 2650–2350 BCE
Earthenware

Bowl

China, ca. 3200–2650 BCE
Earthenware

Vase for Multiple Offerings (Kernos)

Cyclades, ca. 2300–2200 BCE
Terracotta

Terracotta Rhyton

Greece, ca. 460 BCE
Terracotta

Jar Decorated with Animals and Human Figures

Egypt, ca. 3500–3300 BCE
Pottery

Krater

Greece, 750–735 BCE
Terracotta

Clay Tablet Recording a Loan of Silver

Turkey, ca. 20th–19th century BCE
Clay

CLAY

Clay is one of Earth's most abundant substances, and it was widely available in the ancient world. When combined with water, clay can be modeled or molded into different shapes, and it hardens when the water evaporates. When heated at high temperatures in a fire pit or (from around 5000 BCE in Mesopotamia and the Near East) fired in a kiln, clay becomes a much harder and more durable ceramic object. The marks you can see on the cooking pot from Japan show that it had cords tied around it before it was lowered into a fire pit. The rest of the objects pictured here would have been made in a kiln. Clay was used to make objects from vessels to figurines as well as writing tablets that fit into the palm of a hand, like the one from Turkey on the opposite page. Ceramic objects could be glazed or painted. Many of the examples shown here are painted with geometric or animal designs.

Storage Jar Decorated with Mountain Goats
Iran, ca. 4000–3600 BCE
Ceramic

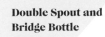

Double Spout and Bridge Bottle
Paracas, 7th–5th century BCE
Ceramic

Cup with Geometric Decoration
Iran, ca. 4500–4100 BCE
Ceramic

PAINT

The first paints were made by mixing minerals ground into a powder (or pigment) with substances like animal fat or plant sap. This paint was applied to rocks by hand or with a stick. Later, painters across the ancient world used not only mineral pigments but also dye-based pigments (like indigo and madder) and synthetic pigments (like Egyptian blue and Han blue). The Egyptian ceiling painting on the left, from the palace complex of Amenhotep III at Malqata, was painted on mud plaster. Later, wall paintings known as frescoes were made by applying paint directly to wet plaster, as in the two wall paintings below, one of which is from the Roman villa at Boscoreale and the other from the Mexican city of Teotihuacán.

Ceiling Painting from the Palace of Amenhotep III
Egypt, ca. 1390–1353 BCE
Paint on mud plaster

Wall Painting
Rome, ca. 50–40 BCE
Fresco

Wall Painting
Teotihuacán, Mexico, 500–550 CE
Paint on plaster

Did you know?

Paints were also made by adding egg or wax to pigment. The addition of egg made quick-drying paint known as egg tempera. Encaustic was a painting technique that used pigment mixed with beeswax, as in this Egyptian painting of a teenage boy named Eutyches.

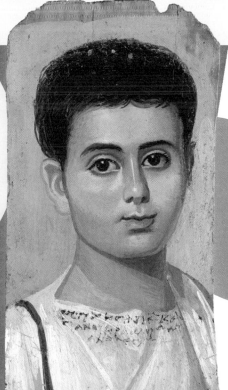

Portrait of the Boy Eutyches
Egypt, 100–150 CE
Encaustic on wood

False Door of the Royal Sealer Neferiu
Egypt, ca. 2150–2010 BCE
Painted limestone

Wall Painting Fragment
Roman, 1st century CE
Fresco

Wall Painting Fragment
Roman, 1st century CE
Fresco

Artist's Sketch of a Pharaoh Spearing a Lion
Egypt, ca. 1186–1070 BCE
Ink on limestone

Wall Painting Fragment
Roman, 1st century CE
Fresco

Wall Painting Fragment
Roman, 1st century CE
Fresco

Did you know?

Different cultures developed unique ways of spinning and weaving. Cloth could be made from many materials. For example, strands of animal hair were used to make warm fiber (sheep and goats were domesticated in West Asia about 10,000 years ago for fiber production). In Egypt, fine linen was spun from flax fibers, while cotton was produced in many places across the world, including the Indus Valley. In Asia, delicate silk was made from the thread produced by silk moths.

Thigh Guard

Greece, ca. 510–500 BCE
Terracotta

This thigh guard would have been worn by women preparing wool for spinning.

Weavers, Tomb of Khnumhotep

Egypt, 1931 CE; original ca. 1897–1878 BCE

This copy of a scene painted on the walls of the tomb of Khnumhotep depicts a group of weavers.

Linen

Egypt, ca. 1492–1473 BCE

Cosmetic Jar Sealed with Linen

Egypt, ca. 1897–1878 BCE

CLOTH

Look at the scene depicted on the Greek oil flask to the left. The women in the center are working on an upright loom, passing their shuttles through the vertical strands of wool. The vase also shows women weighing wool and spinning it into yarn by twisting fibers together to make a strong thread. Objects like this vase—and the spindle whorls and weaving tools on this page—give us a sense of how ancient cloth was made.

Although textiles deteriorate due to moisture, biological activity, and other factors, objects like the colorful textiles from Peru pictured below have survived due in part to the dry, hot desert air. Carefully wrapped and preserved, they were buried with their owners.

Terracotta Lekythos (Oil Flask)
Greece, ca. 550-530 BCE

Loom Weight
Greece, ca. 575-525 BCE
Terracotta

Tunic with Confronting Catfish
Peru, 800-850 CE
Camelid hair

Weaving Tool
Egypt, ca. 1295-1070 BCE
Bone

Ball of Weaving Thread
Egypt, ca. 1295-1070 BCE
Linen fiber

Spindle with Whorl
Egypt, ca. 1295-1070 BCE
Wood

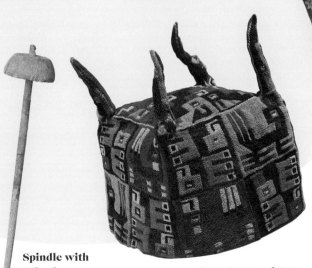

Four-Cornered Hat
Peru, 500-900 CE
Camelid fiber

Belt
Peru, 200-700 CE
Camelid fiber

PAPER

Thousands of years ago, the ancient Egyptians began to use papyrus for writing and recording information. Like papyrus, paper today is made from plant fibers. Papyrus was made from papyrus plants that grew along the River Nile. The core of the stalk was cut into thin strips that were laid out in two layers and then pressed together. A freshly finished papyrus sheet was often smoothed with a burnisher, like the one on the opposite page. Paper is fragile, and only a fraction of the ancient documents written on papyrus or parchment (stretched animal skin) scrolls have survived. However, some important texts like the Egyptian Book of the Dead papyri, which contain spells and prayers, were sealed in tombs, which helped preserve them. The Dead Sea Scrolls, ancient religious writings, were found tightly sealed in clay jars, like the one shown opposite, which preserved them for thousands of years until they were discovered in caves in the 1940s.

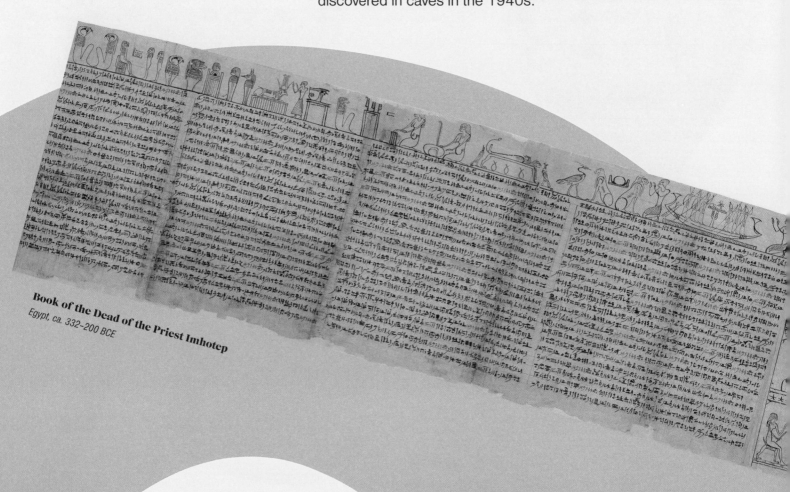

Book of the Dead of the Priest Imhotep
Egypt, ca. 332–200 BCE

Did you know?

The Greeks wrote on papyrus too! The fragment pictured below includes lines from the *Odyssey*, a text attributed to the Greek author Homer. The Great Library of Alexandria in Egypt collected writings from across the Mediterranean and was home to hundreds of thousands of scrolls.

Papyrus Marsh
*Egypt, 1914–1916 CE,
original ca. 1427–1400 BCE*

**Heqanakht
Letter V**
Egypt, ca. 1961–1917 BCE

**Papyrus Fragment
with Lines from
Homer's Odyssey**
Greece, ca. 285–250 BCE

**Dead Sea Scroll
Jar and Lid**
Qumran, ca. 2nd century BCE

Papyrus Burnisher
Egypt, ca. 1981–1802 BCE

**Fragment of the Gospel
of St. John 2:11-22**
Egypt, 4th century

Ancient Mesopotamia

From around 3500 BCE, Mesopotamia, present-day Iraq, with its sun, the Tigris and Euphrates rivers, and mineral-rich soil, was home to some of the world's first cities and states. The people of these communities created systems that allowed them to invent, craft, and trade. Cities grew in size and population, and new ones sprang up. Their trade networks stretched as far east as the Indus Valley, in present-day Pakistan and northwestern India, west to the Nile Valley in Egypt, and later across the Mediterranean Sea.

Standing Male Worshiper

Iraq, ca. 2900–2600 BCE

Standing Female Worshiper

Iraq, ca. 2600–2500 BCE

These stone worshiper figures stand with their hands clasped together in a position of prayer. Figures like these not only were images of people but could act for them in certain ways, and were placed in temples to worship the gods on behalf of the person they represented. Some statues were even believed to be inhabited by gods themselves.

Sumer

The Sumerians lived in southern Mesopotamia (modern-day Iraq). They built some of the world's first cities, including Uruk, which was already a big city before 3000 BCE, and developed technologies like writing, which helped large numbers of people live and work together.

Cylinder Seals

Many people carried small stones that today we call cylinder seals. A seal was carved in reverse, so that the intended image would appear as an impression when it was rolled over damp clay. The impression on clay could act as a mark of ownership or as a person's signature on a letter or contract.

Cylinder Seal and Modern Impression: Hunting Scene

Iraq, ca. 2250–2150 BCE

This stone cylinder seal shows a hunting scene. The impression on the right shows the raised design that appears when the seal is rolled over wet clay.

Molded Plaque: Couple

Iraq, 2000–1700 BCE

This plaque, almost 4,000 years old, shows two figures holding one another and looking into each other's eyes. We can still recognize them today as a couple in love.

Babylonia

Babylonia was a kingdom in ancient southern Iraq. Its capital, the city of Babylon, was rebuilt on a grand scale by King Nebuchadnezzar II (reigned ca. 604–562 BCE). Colorful animal sculptures made from glazed bricks lined the city's walls. For centuries, Babylon was one of the world's largest cities, but over time, other cities in central Iraq took on its role in politics and trade. One of these, Baghdad, was founded in the 8th century and is still Iraq's capital today.

Assyria

The kings of Assyria ruled northern Iraq, and sometimes a much larger region stretching from Iraq to the Mediterranean Sea, from ca. 1500–612 BCE, and built the cities of Nineveh, Nimrud, and Khorsabad. Their images survive today in grand stone carvings that lined the walls of their palaces.

Relief Panel

Iraq, ca. 883–859 BCE

This relief carving is from the palace of Ashurnasirpal II at Nimrud. The king, on the left, wears a distinctive headdress and fine jewelry. Reliefs like this appear as plain stone today, but tiny traces of paint reveal that they were originally brightly colored. The horizontal markings running across the figures just below their waists are a written inscription in cuneiform, a type of script, that lists the achievements of Ashurnasirpal II.

Great Cities

The cities of the Ancient Near East, such as Ur, Nineveh, and Babylon, were built and rebuilt by different leaders over the years. These cities were surrounded by walls that kept intruders out. Inside were temples where the gods were honored and palaces from which leaders ruled their kingdoms.

Human-Headed Winged Bull

Iraq, ca. 883-859 BCE

Nimrud was made the capital city of the Assyrian Empire by King Ashurnasirpal II, who completely rebuilt it, constructing city walls, temples, and a fine palace. In its doorways stood fantastic sculptures expertly carved in stone—part animal, part human—with heads, wings, hooves, and tails. This guardian figure has five legs because it was designed to be viewed from both the front and the side.

Cities and Architecture

Towering mountainlike structures called ziggurats were built in city centers; the ziggurat of Ur was constructed around 2100 BCE. Ziggurats were made of mud bricks arranged in a series of stepped platforms. At the top were temples where priests performed rituals and made offerings to the gods. Nearby, great palaces were filled with fine furniture and textiles, though because of the materials in which they were made, these have often not survived. In Assyria, palace walls were lined with relief sculptures that showed their leaders' achievements and victories in battle.

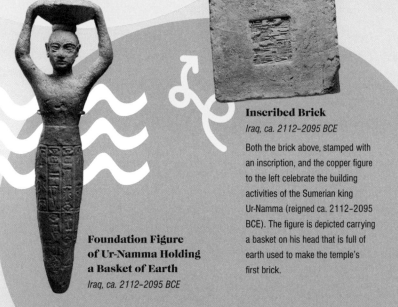

Foundation Figure of Ur-Namma Holding a Basket of Earth

Iraq, ca. 2112-2095 BCE

Inscribed Brick

Iraq, ca. 2112-2095 BCE

Both the brick above, stamped with an inscription, and the copper figure to the left celebrate the building activities of the Sumerian king Ur-Namma (reigned ca. 2112–2095 BCE). The figure is depicted carrying a basket on his head that is full of earth used to make the temple's first brick.

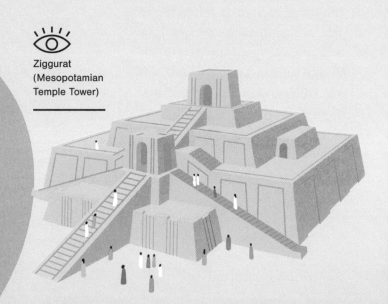

Ziggurat (Mesopotamian Temple Tower)

Artisans in Ancient Mesopotamia

Craftspeople in these cities worked in groups to make cloth, pottery, tools, religious objects, and architectural ornaments. Some of these objects were made specifically for the afterlife. Archaeologists have found precious jewelry, sculptures, and musical instruments buried in graves or in the walls and floors of temples and palaces.

Relief Fragment: Cavalry Men Along a Stream in Mountainous Terrain
Iraq, ca. 704-681 BCE

This panel was originally part of a huge wall relief in a palace at Nineveh in northern Iraq built by the Assyrian king Sennacherib (r. ca. 704-681 BCE). It shows soldiers leading their horses through a mountain landscape, possibly the Zagros Mountains in Iran, as part of an Assyrian military campaign. The relief includes stylized representations of a flowing stream (wavy lines under the soldiers' feet) and a mountain landscape (the curved pattern of the background) and would once have been brightly painted.

Cuneiform Cylinder Describing the Construction of the Outer City Wall of Babylon
Iraq, ca. 604-562 BCE

Babylon had been a major city since the reign of King Hammurabi (r. ca. 1792-1750 BCE). This clay cylinder, inscribed in cuneiform script and buried in the foundations of the city of Babylon, describes a grand building project of King Nebuchadnezzar II (r. ca. 604-562 BCE).

Panel with Striding Lion
Iraq, ca. 604-562 BCE

This is one of many similar glazed brick panels from the grandest street in Babylon, the Processional Way. Lions like this lined the route for ritual processions from the inner city out through the Ishtar Gate to a temple called Bit Akitu, or "House of the New Year's Festival." The Ishtar Gate, built by King Nebuchadnezzar II, was a glazed-brick structure dedicated to Ishtar, the goddess of love and war. The striding lions—the animal associated with the goddess—were thought to protect the street.

Early Writing

The people living across the Ancient Near East developed a system of writing called cuneiform, which they used first for business and later for recording poems and stories.

Proto Cuneiform Tablet with Seal Impression

Iraq, ca. 3100–2900 BCE

This tablet contains pictographs. It is a record of grain, probably the grain distributed by a large temple. The round dots represent numbers.

Cuneiform Writing

As cities grew, it became necessary to produce written records. Trained scribes wrote using a cut reed, which they pressed into a tablet made of soft clay; the clay could be smoothed over and reused, or sun-dried or baked to keep the writing forever. Most tablets were small and gently curved so that they fit into the palm of the writer's hand. Early tablets contained images called pictographs (pictures that represented objects or ideas). They recorded basic information about crops that had been produced and goods that were bought and sold.

Over time, pictographs developed into cuneiform, a system of writing used to record at least 15 languages across the region. Written with characters made up of wedges, which stood for individual sounds as well as words, it was in use for more than 3,000 years—and not just for business. Histories, poems to the gods, and great stories like the epic tale of Gilgamesh were all recorded in cuneiform. The Assyrian king Ashurbanipal (r. 669–631 BCE) kept a library of more than 30,000 tablets.

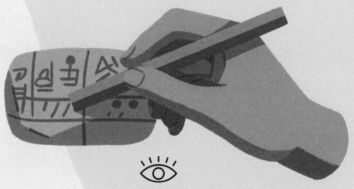

Clay tablets were inscribed with a cut reed.

Cuneiform Tablet: Hymn

Iraq, 1st millennium BCE

This clay tablet is inscribed with a hymn celebrating Marduk, an important god honored by the Babylonians. The text is written here in two languages: Sumerian and Akkadian.

Cuneiform Tablet: List of Magical Stones

Iraq, mid- to late 1st millennium BCE

This tablet forms part of a description of 303 stones that could be used to treat different medical conditions. These stones might have been used in a variety of ways. Some were worn on the body as amulets. The stones of cylinder seals might also have been used in this way.

Agriculture and Animal Symbolism

Using new tools and methods, Ancient Near Eastern people increased crop production and transformed farming. Domesticated and wild animals were important resources but also had symbolic meanings and were depicted in many religious, ritual, and funerary objects.

Bull's Head: Ornament for a Lyre

Iraq, ca. 2600–2350 BCE

This finely crafted bronze bull's head was once attached to a lyre—a stringed musical instrument played at royal celebrations. The bull looks straight at us with eyes made of a deep-blue gem called lapis lazuli, set in shell.

Kneeling Bull Holding a Spouted Vessel

Iran, ca. 3100–2900 BCE

Representations of humanlike animals appeared in the Proto-Elamite period (ca. 3100–2700 BCE). We do not know who or what the kneeling bull represents or how this object was used, but traces of cloth found on its surface suggest that it was deliberately buried as part of a ritual or ceremony.

Figure of a Man with an Oryx, a Monkey, and a Leopard Skin

Iraq, ca. 800 BCE

This carved ivory figure is one of a group that seems to represent figures bringing gifts or tribute to the king of Assyria. He carries a leopardskin draped across his shoulder and grips the horns of an oryx (desert antelope), while a monkey sits on his shoulder.

Storage Jar Decorated with Mountain Goats

Iran, ca. 4000–3600 BCE

This storage jar is a masterpiece of early pottery making. The stylized design includes dynamic, geometric patterns. Three main panels around the jar show ibexes (a kind of wild mountain goat) with enormous ridged horns. The bodies and horns of the goats form circles, making them both images of animals and part of the pattern.

Art Making

Some ancient craftspeople excelled in metalwork and created fine tools and pieces of jewelry. Gold was heated, hammered, coiled, and fashioned into precious ornaments, necklaces, earrings, rings, and pendants; sculptures were carved in stone or ivory or cast in metal.

Headdress
Iraq, ca. 2600–2500 BCE

The delicate gold leaves in this headpiece are separated by blue (lapis lazuli) and red (carnelian) gemstone beads. Headdresses like this were placed on the heads of female attendants buried with royal men and women in the city of Ur. Gold, lapis lazuli, and carnelian are not found in Mesopotamia and had to be imported over long distances.

Art and Trade

Works of art found across the Ancient Near East make it clear that there was a great trade network stretching east and west. Items like the headdress, below, that are made from materials not found in Mesopotamia are evidence of strong trade networks and royal wealth. A single piece of jewelry might include gold from Egypt or Anatolia, precious stone like lapis lazuli from the mountains of Afghanistan, and ivory from elephants hunted in southern Egypt or Syria. People traded in finished objects as well as raw materials.

Fitting the Mold

An important technique invented at this time (and still used today) is the lost wax method. To make a metal object using this method, the artisan would first make a model in beeswax. They would then cover the wax model in clay, leaving a few holes in the clay covering. The clay was placed in a fire to harden, and the hot, melted wax inside would drain out through the holes. Molten metal (such as liquid bronze—a mixture of copper and tin) would be poured into the holes; it would cool and harden inside the clay, taking the shape of the now "lost" wax model. Artisans would then break the clay mold to reveal the final metal sculpture.

Striding Figure with Ibex Horns, a Raptor Skin Draped Around the Shoulders, and Upturned Boots
Iran, ca. 3000 BCE

This booted figure wears a headdress of horns and has the wings of a bird of prey draped around his shoulders. Sculpted in copper alloy, he is an early example of the lost wax method of casting.

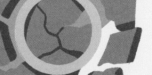

The final step in the lost wax method was to break the clay mold to reveal the final sculpture.

**Chair Back with
a Tree Pattern**
Iraq, ca. 800–700 BCE

Carved Ivories

These pieces of carved ivory were among a huge collection discovered in the royal palaces at Nimrud in Iraq. Each fragment formed part of a piece of furniture. Some still show traces of gold, glass, or precious stones. Lifelike animals, fantastic creatures, plants, and flowers were all popular subjects.

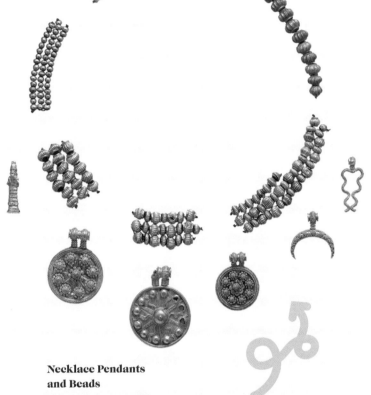

**Necklace Pendants
and Beads**

Iraq, 18th–17th century BCE

The seven gold pendants in this collection of gold beads represent different gods and goddesses. The two female figures on the left wear horned headdresses and long flounced dresses. They probably represent Lama, a protective goddess. The disk with rays in the center represents Shamash, the sun god, and the two other round pendants may be symbols of Ishtar, goddess of love and war, who was associated with the planet Venus. The lunar crescent is a symbol of the moon god Sin, and the forked lightning on the right is a symbol for Adad, the storm god.

**Furniture Plaque Carved
in Relief with a Striding,
Ram-Headed Sphinx Supported
by Two Kneeling Figures**
Iraq, ca. 9th–8th century BCE

The tabs at the top and bottom of this plaque were originally used to set the ivory into wooden furniture.

**Openwork Furniture Plaque
with Two Sphinxes**
Syria, ca. 9th–8th century BCE

This carved ivory sphinx figure was probably from ancient Hadatu, now the town of Arslan Tash in northern Syria. Tiny traces of gold are still visible on the figure's Egyptian-style headdress and collar.

Storytelling

Assyrian palace walls were lined with stone relief carvings. Many told stories that glorified important victories in war or success in ritual royal hunts. Some images included text (written using cuneiform script, in the Akkadian language) that provided more detail about the events shown or the king who had commissioned them.

Reliefs

Reliefs were carved stone panels that formed part of a building—a wall, a frieze, or a door. They would originally have been painted in bright colors to create a bold and eye-catching display. Traces of paint still remain on some of the figures. Today, scientists can study these traces to learn more about what the object might have looked like when it was fully painted.

Relief Panels from Nimrud

Iraq, ca. 883–859 BCE

These two relief panels from the Assyrian palace at Nimrud show protective winged figures that fuse human and animal forms and are inscribed in cuneiform script with details of the achievements of Ashurnasipal II. The figures may have been made to purify and protect the palace by keeping out demons and harmful spirits.

Battle Scene of Assyrians Storming a City
Iraq, 704–681 BCE

This relief is from the walls of a royal palace at Nineveh.
The palace contains works commissioned by many different rulers
over the years. This fragment is from the reign of Sennacherib and
shows rows of Assyrian soldiers attacking a fortified city. Archers
fire arrows, and soldiers ascend a steep ramp.

Orthostat Relief: Winged Human-Headed Lion
Syria, ca. 10th–9th century BCE

Relief blocks like this, from Tell Halaf on the border
between Syria and Turkey, are closely related to the
Assyrian palace carvings. This example shows a fantastic
winged creature with a lion's body, a human face, and
the horned crown associated with divine beings.

Ancient Egypt

Egypt is a country in the northeast of Africa. The River Nile, which is the longest river in Africa, flows through the country. The ancient Egyptian civilization lasted for 3,500 years, from about 3100 BCE to about 400 CE. We can tell a lot about ancient Egypt's people and their beliefs from the many objects that survive.

Egyptian Rulers

Large statues of the pharaohs, Egypt's rulers, were carved in stone. Pharaohs were often depicted sitting on a throne or wearing distinctive headdresses. Hieroglyphic inscriptions on these statues often give their name and royal titles.

Seated Statue of Hatshepsut
Egypt, ca. 1479–1458 BCE

Hatshepsut was an important female pharaoh who ruled Egypt about 3,500 years ago. She's pictured sitting on a throne.

Queen Nefertari Playing Senet
1921–22 CE; original Egypt, ca. 1279–1213 BCE

Nefertari was the wife of Pharaoh Ramesses II. This is a copy of one of the elaborate paintings in her tomb. She is wearing a vulture headdress—which is only worn by royal women and goddesses—and is playing a game called Senet.

Senwosret III as a Sphinx
Egypt, ca. 1878–1840 BCE

King Senwosret III is shown here as a sphinx—a figure with the body of a lion and head of a man. Crouching sphinx figures were positioned to guard sacred places.

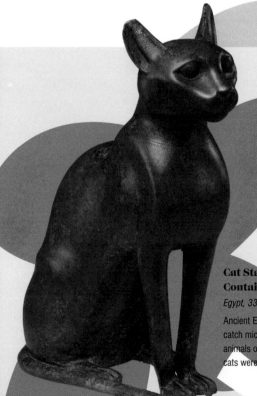

Animals

Ancient Egyptians encountered many animals in their daily lives. They often associated a specific animal with a specific god (or sometimes several gods).

Cat Statuette Intended to Contain a Mummified Cat
Egypt, 332–330 BCE

Ancient Egyptians kept cats as pets and to catch mice. They were considered the sacred animals of the goddess Bastet. Mummified cats were given as gifts to the goddess.

Cosmetic Dish in the Shape of a Bolti Fish
Egypt, ca. 1479–1425 BCE

This engraved stone dish is modeled in the shape of the bolti fish, known for carrying and hatching eggs in its mouth.

Block with Pharaoh Mentuhotep II

Egypt, ca. 2010–2000 BCE

This carved relief shows Mentuhotep II, a pharaoh who united Egypt. Two of his names are written in oval-shaped rings called cartouches. The goddess figure on the right was chiseled away during the rule of Akhenaten (1352–1336 BCE); he wanted people to focus on one god, Aten.

King Sahure Accompanied by a Divine Figure

Egypt, 2458–2446 BCE

The small figure on the left is handing the King an ankh symbol, indicating life. Ancient Egyptians believed that the gods had the power to give life.

Did you know?

The ankh symbol is the ancient Egyptian sign of life. It was used as a hieroglyph to represent the word "live," "alive," or "life." This one was found in the tomb of King Thutmose IV.

Head of Tutankhamun

Egypt, ca. 1336–1327 BCE

This head of the boy-king Tutankhamun was once part of a larger statue. The statue showed Tutankhamen in front of a god. All that remains of the god is the huge hand.

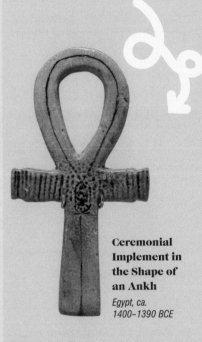

Ceremonial Implement in the Shape of an Ankh

Egypt, ca. 1400–1390 BCE

Inlay Depicting a Falcon with Spread Wings

Egypt, 4th century BCE

This falcon represents the god Horus. The falcon, with its outstretched wings offering protection, is often pictured above the head of a king.

Hippopotamus ("William")

Egypt, ca. 1961–1878 BCE

Some of the most dangerous creatures the Egyptians encountered were the hippopotamuses that lived in the River Nile. This sculpture, made from faience and decorated with lotus flowers, has been known as "William" since a story about him appeared in a 1931 magazine article.

Life on the Nile

In the Nile valley, farmers raised and kept animals, including cattle, sheep, and goats. They hunted, fished, and farmed crops like barley and wheat. Every year, the Nile River flooded, bringing water and rich deposits of fertile dark silt to the surrounding lands.

Model of a Man Plowing
Egypt, ca. 1981–1885 BCE

This painted wooden model, discovered in a tomb, shows two oxen pulling a plow across a field, with a farmer standing behind them. The plow was an important invention that allowed seeds to be planted more efficiently in the soil.

Nikare as a Scribe
Egypt, ca. 2420–2389 BCE or later

The scribe Nikare is depicted here holding a papyrus scroll in his lap. He's shown with folded legs, the typical pose of a scribe.

Menna and Family Hunting in the Marshes
Egypt, 1924 CE; original ca. 1400–1352 BCE

This is a copy of a wall painting from the tomb of Menna, an important Egyptian official. He is pictured twice (left and right), standing on a papyrus boat called a skiff. On the right, surrounded by his family, he is poised to catch fish, while on the left, he is hunting birds. The scene is filled with bird and animal life.

Activities

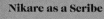

The people of the Nile valley were involved in many different occupations. Officials carried out the pharaoh's orders. Scribes were important figures in the community. Reading and writing weren't common; only some could receive this special training.

Hairpin Decorated with a Cobra
Egypt, ca. 1783–1640 BCE

The top of this ivory hairpin is carved in the shape of a cobra wearing a crown.

Kohl Tube
Egypt, ca. 1295–1070 BCE

This tube shows the Egyptians' expertise in glass-making. It was made to hold kohl, dark black powder made from ground minerals, mixed with oils or animal fats, and used as eye makeup.

Dressing Up

Egyptians wore dresses, loincloths, and kilts made of linen and used perfumes, cosmetics, and other accessories to keep themselves looking good—in life and in death.

Amenemhat's Razor
Egypt, ca. 1504–1447 BCE

This metal razor was found in the coffin of Amenemhat. Many Egyptians, particularly priests, shaved their heads.

Comb
Egypt, ca. 1550–1458 BCE

This wooden hair comb was found in a tomb. It is very well preserved.

Gods and Goddesses

Egyptians sought the protection of many gods and goddesses. Individual gods could take on multiple different appearances and were often depicted with the body of a human and the head of an animal. Egyptian deities were worshiped in temples, where special rituals were performed. People used charms and spells to invoke their help, and gods and goddesses also had particular roles in the afterlife.

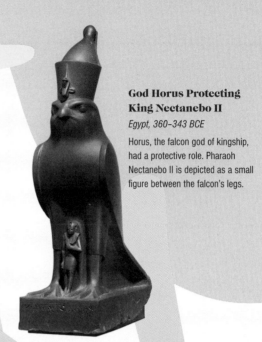

God Horus Protecting King Nectanebo II
Egypt, 360–343 BCE

Horus, the falcon god of kingship, had a protective role. Pharaoh Nectanebo II is depicted as a small figure between the falcon's legs.

Head of the God Amun
Egypt, ca. 1336–1327 BCE

Amun, god of the air, can be recognized as a god by his braided beard, part of which has broken off this statue. This statue shows the remains of his beard and his hat with two vertical plumes, which have also broken off. It was created for Amun's vast temple at Karnak.

Thoth
Egypt, 332–30 BCE

Thoth, god of writing and wisdom, was associated with the ibis bird and the baboon. In this blue faience sculpture, he's pictured with an ibis's head.

Nephthys Amulet

Egypt, 332–30 BCE

Nephthys was the sister of Isis. She was known as protector of the dead. The hieroglyphs on her head give her name.

Isis and Horus

Egypt, 664–30 BCE

Isis, the wife of the god Osiris, is often pictured with their child, Horus, on her lap. It's believed that the Christian Virgin and Child are connected with this image.

Hathor Head Jewelry Spacer

Egypt, 664–332 BCE

Hathor, goddess of motherhood and fertility, is often pictured as a cow, or with a cow's ears.

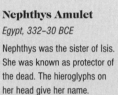

Protective Wand

Egypt, ca. 1981–1640 BCE

This wand was carved from the tooth of a hippopotamus. Decorated with many protective figures, wands like these probably offered protection during childbirth. They were also placed in tombs to help with rebirth.

Charms

The Egyptians believed that objects could be bestowed with magical powers. The selection of charms and spells presented here were designed to protect their owners.

Magical Container in the Shape of a Hippopotamus Deity

Egypt, ca. 1700–1500 BCE

This lidded container may have contained a papyrus charm with a spell to protect mother and child during childbirth.

Baby's Feeding Cup

Egypt, ca. 1850–1700 BCE

Like the wand above, this cup—shaped to feed a baby—is decorated with animals that were thought to offer magical protection.

Magical Stela

Egypt, 360–343 BCE

A stela is a carved or painted slab of stone or wood. This stone stela is engraved with 13 spells and a story about the god Horus. The texts and images on this stela were meant to cure or protect against the illnesses caused by poisonous bites. It was placed in the public part of a temple. Patients could visit to drink water that had been poured over the stela to absorb its healing powers.

Making Art

Paintings from Egyptian tombs show us craftspeople at work and give us a great sense of how works of art were made. While working out large-scale wall paintings, artists produced ink sketches on pieces of limestone; these are known as *ostraka*.

Did you know?

In paintings, artists depicted people with their face in profile, but the eye front-on. Their torso was in profile, but their shoulders were front-on.

The god Anubis

Sculptors at Work, Tomb of Rekhmire
Egypt, ca. 1479–1425 BCE

These sculptors are pictured working on a colossal statue—chiseling, sanding, and painting. This is a copy of a wall painting from the tomb of Rekhmire, an important official.

Striding Figure
Egypt, ca. 2575–2465 BCE

This figure, who is shown with clenched fists and one leg forward, is made from a hard stone called quartzite. Traces of paint still remain, which suggest that he once had a mustache and was wearing a large necklace.

Craftsmen, Tomb of Nebamun and Ipuky
Egypt, ca. 1921 CE; original 1390–1349 BCE

These workers are painting, chiseling, and carving a variety of objects. They are overseen by a supervisor, the large figure on the left, who is also the deceased. The picture is a copy of a wall painting from the Tomb of Nebamun and Ipuky.

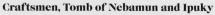

Faience

Many Egyptian objects were made from a material known as faience. This was made from a mix of sand or ground quartz, salts, lime, and colorants, such as copper minerals. These were ground into a fine powder, mixed with water to create a thick paste, and shaped by hand or with clay molds. When the objects were fired, a chemical reaction turned them the desired color—often bright blue-green. Faience was widely used to make amulets and figures known as shabtis.

Shabti of Seti I

Egypt, ca. 1294–1279 BCE

This shabti was one of hundreds made for Pharaoh Seti I, the father of Ramesses II. Shabtis were substitute figures placed in tombs. Their job was to perform tasks for the owner in the afterlife.

Marsh Bowl

Egypt, ca. 1550–1458 BCE

This large faience bowl is decorated with lotus flowers—blooms that close at night and open during the day, symbolizing rebirth. They radiate from a rectangle in the center of the bowl, which represents a pond.

Sphinx of Amenhotep III

Egypt, ca. 1390–1352 BCE

This faience sphinx has a particularly bright, even blue glaze. It has the body of a lion but a human head, arms, and hands.

Architecture

The Egyptians built monumental stone temples to honor their gods and huge tomb complexes where royals and important officials were buried. Temples were considered to be the homes of the gods and were looked after by priests who performed rituals there, which included making offerings of food and drink and burning incense. Many tombs consisted of an underground burial chamber and above it a chapel where offerings were made by the deceased's family.

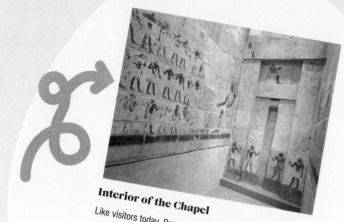

Interior of the Chapel

Like visitors today, Perneb's family entered the chapel through a narrow opening that led to a corridor and a small room filled with painted relief carvings. A false door made of stone represents a real doorway—it was believed that Perneb's spirit would pass through the chapel and receive the food and drink left for him.

Figure Carrying an Offering in the Temple of Perneb

Egypt, 2381–2323 BCE

The walls of the chapel are filled with painted reliefs. This figure is bringing an animal as a food offering to Perneb.

Tomb of Perneb

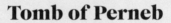

The Tomb of Perneb, excavated from the ancient cemetery of Saqqara, was the burial place of Perneb, an important Egyptian official. Perneb was responsible for dressing the king and taking care of his clothing and equipment. Perneb's body had been placed in an underground chamber beneath a richly decorated tomb chapel, where his family brought offerings.

Temple of Dendur

The Temple of Dendur, from Nubia, was created by the Roman Emperor Augustus, when Egypt was part of the Roman Empire. The temple was mainly dedicated to the goddess Isis. She is featured in the pictures carved in relief on the walls, along with her husband Osiris, son Horus, and many other gods and goddesses. Images of papyrus and lotus plants decorate the temple and its central columns.

Scenes from the Southern Wall of the Temple of Dendur

Egypt, completed by 10 BCE

The Roman Emperor Augustus, who ruled Egypt from 27 BCE to 14 CE, is pictured on the temple walls, dressed as a pharaoh, making offerings to different Egyptian gods and goddesses, including Osiris and Horus. These images would have been painted in bright colors.

Art for the Afterlife

The ancient Egyptians believed that life continued after death. Tombs were filled with all the objects that would be required in the next life. Detailed rituals ensured the everlasting life of the deceased. For example, to make sure that the deceased had food in the next life, prayers for food were made, food was depicted on the walls of the tomb, and real food was placed inside the tomb. In this way, there were several layers to ensure that the deceased had the foodstuff they needed.

Did you know?

During mummification, Egyptians usually left the heart in the body. They believed that it was central to a person and was the place where memories were stored. Egyptians believed that the heart would be weighed after death to assess whether they had been a good person and could pass through into the afterlife.

Funerary Mask of the Overseer of Builders, Amenhotep
Egypt, ca. 1427–1390 BCE
Masks like these covered the head of the deceased. This one is made from painted cartonnage (linen or papyrus mixed with plaster) and is gilded. Royal masks were made of gold.

Coffin of Henettawy
Egypt, ca. 1000–945 BCE
Henettawy was a musician for the god Amun-Ra. This coffin is covered with images of gods and goddesses who will protect her in the next life.

Mummification

Preserving the body by mummification included removing its organs and storing them in canopic jars. The body was covered with natron to dry it out and stop it from rotting. It was then wrapped in linen and placed in a coffin, which was often decorated with writing and images.

Stela of Aafenmut

Egypt, ca. 924–889 BCE

Painted stelae often included prayers. This one shows Aafenmut offering incense, bread, fruit, and flowers to the falcon-headed sun god, Re-Harakhty.

Heart Scarab of Hatnefer

Egypt, ca. 1492–1473 BCE

Heart scarabs were popular amulets, placed in the bandages of mummified individuals. Their flat undersides were usually inscribed with a spell from the *Book of the Dead*. This one was found in the tomb of Hatnefer.

Model of a Procession of Offering Bearers

Egypt, ca. 1981–1975 BCE

In this wooden model from the tomb of high-ranking official Meketre, figures who are probably his family are shown carrying offerings of an incense burner, linen sheets, and food.

The Afterlife

Egyptians believed that after death, a person would travel to the afterlife. To help the deceased navigate through the underworld, tombs often contained texts and images that were thought to guide them, such as maps or magical spells. The *Book of the Dead* is the most famous text. It is a guide through the underworld, complete with spells.

Loaf of Bread

Egypt, ca. 1492–1473 BCE

This loaf of bread and dish of raisins are real food, not sculptures! They were placed as offerings in the tomb of Hatnefer.

Bowl of Raisins

Egypt, ca. 1492–1473 BCE

Ancient Greece

The islands of the Aegean Sea, and the land surrounding it, were home to many different groups of people. Unique cultures, each with their own particular styles of art, sprang up across the region. Over several thousand years, trade and travel brought people into closer contact. Eventually, the many Greek city-states were united as part of the Macedonian Empire under Alexander the Great (r. 336–323 BCE).

Marble Seated Harp Player
Cycladic, 2800–2700 BCE

This ancient marble sculpture of a harp player from the Cycladic islands is one of the earliest surviving images of a musician. The instrument looks as if it's an extension of the figure's body.

Early Art

Some of the earliest surviving art of Greece is from the Cycladic Islands, where marble figures were carved from about 4500 BCE. Painting and pottery also flourished in the Minoan civilization, which prospered on the island of Crete between about 2200 and 1450 BCE. Gold and pottery treasures have been found in the remains of the palace of Mycenae on the Greek mainland; the Mycenaean civilization peaked about 1250 BCE.

Terracotta Stirrup Jar with Octopus
Mycenaean, ca. 1200–1100 BCE

Like the Minoans, the Mycenaeans covered jars with geometric patterns and images of sea creatures like this octopus, whose eight tentacles swirl around its curved body.

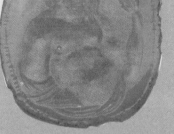

Carnelian Engraved Gem with a Portrait of Socrates

Roman, ca. 1st century BCE–1st century CE

This Roman gemstone was carved with a portrait of the bearded Greek philosopher Socrates, who lived in Athens in about 470–399 BCE.

Did you know?

The ancient Greeks are known for creating an alphabet that is still used today. They are also known for the system of democracy (rule by the people), which was used to govern the city of Athens, home to philosophers and writers. The Greeks are also remembered for sporting competitions that were the forerunners of today's Olympic Games.

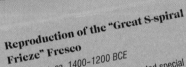

Reproduction of the "Great S-spiral Frieze" Fresco

Mycenaean, ca. 1400–1200 BCE

The Minoans and Mycenaeans decorated special buildings with brightly colored frescoes—pictures painted directly onto the walls' wet plaster. This reconstruction was recreated from fragments discovered in the Mycenaean palace of Tiryns.

Greek Alphabet Polyhedron

Greek, 2nd–1st century BCE

This 20-sided polyhedron has a letter from the 24-letter Greek alphabet on each face, from A (alpha) to Y (upsilon). The last four letters are missing. It would have been thrown to consult an oracle, whose responses were matched to the letter rolled.

Coins

The first coins appeared at the end of the 7th century BCE in the kingdom of Lydia and in Ionia. Nuggets of metal were weighed and stamped. Eventually, coins were minted all across the region.

Gold Stater of Ptolemy I

Greek, ca. 305–284 BCE

Gold Stater

Greek, ca. 330–320 BCE

Gold Stater

Greek, ca. 323–315 BCE

Making Art

Art flourished all over the Greek world, and fine works of pottery and sculpture were made across the Mediterranean. Early pots and sculptures featured geometric shapes, but over time, artists introduced figural decoration. Close links with cities in the East brought in other styles, including images of sphinxes and griffins. From about 600 BCE, sculptures cast in bronze or carved in marble became more lifelike. Two centuries later, sculptors like Praxiteles became famous across the region. Greek pots were also decorated with figures painted in dramatic poses.

Marble Statue of a Kouros (Youth)
Greek, ca. 590–580 BCE

This marble statue, carved in Attica, marked the grave of a young aristocrat. He stands facing forward—one leg in front, arms at his sides—in a pose similar to the ones seen in Egyptian sculpture. His hair is finely patterned.

Bronze Horse
Greek, 8th century BCE

This bronze horse has been assembled from elegant geometric shapes.

Marble Head of a Ptolemaic Queen
Greek, 270–250 BCE

This finely modeled royal head has been identified as Arsinoe II, who ruled Egypt together with her brother, Ptolemy II, who was also her husband. After her death in 270 BCE, she was worshiped as a goddess.

Bronze Statuette of a Veiled and Masked Dancer
Greek, 3rd–2nd century BCE

Greek artists began to show the human body in motion rather than just standing still. This bronze dancer is almost hidden beneath the folds of cloth draped around her body.

Marble Stele (Grave Marker) with a Youth and a Little Girl, and a Capital and Finial in the Form of a Sphinx
Greek, ca. 530 BCE

This tall column, carved in marble, marked the grave of a youth. Although no color is preserved, it would originally have been brightly painted. A sphinx—part human, part lion—stands on top of the stele as a guardian.

Bronze Statuette of Aphrodite
Greek, ca. 150–100 BCE

This bronze statuette was modeled on a marble sculpture of the goddess Aphrodite of Knidos, by the famous sculptor Praxiteles (ca. 350 BCE). He was well known for creating poses like these, with the body twisted to the side and one leg slightly raised.

Terracotta Panathenaic Prize Amphora
Greek, ca. 530 BCE

Amphoras like these, filled with olive oil, were awarded to the winning athletes of the Panathenaic Games. This sports festival was held in Athens every four years. The goddess Athena is shown on one side of the amphora and racing athletes on the other.

Making Pots

Artists flocked to Athens, where hundreds of studios were making pottery modeled in bright-red clay from the surrounding countryside of Attica. The first pots were decorated with scenes from myths and legends, battles, and athletic competitions. Later ones showed scenes of everyday life—craftspeople at work, weaving and spinning, and music-making and merriment. Pots were modeled in many different shapes, large and small. Many were used for storing, mixing, or drinking wine and for holding oil or perfume.

Black-Figure Pots

These pots had figures painted on them in a black glaze before they were fired. They appear as dramatic silhouettes against the bright terracotta background. Details were scratched into the figures with a sharp-pointed tool.

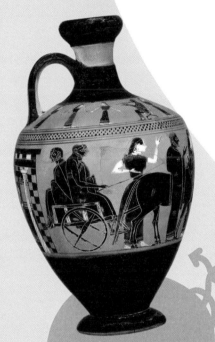

Terracotta Lekythos (Oil Flask)
Greek, ca. 550–530 BCE

Terracotta Bell-Krater
Greek, ca. 440 BCE

Red-Figure Pots

Red-figure pots were produced in Athens from around 530 BCE. They have a glazed black background with figures standing out in bright-red terracotta. Fine details were painted on with a brush before firing.

Terracotta Column-Krater
Greek, ca. 430 BCE

Pots were used to store oil, perfume, or wine.

Storytelling

The Greeks loved telling stories. Their dramatic tales featured gods and goddesses and heroes going off on great adventures. Scenes from these famous stories were celebrated in art, with images of the gods in action painted on fine pots and jars and carved in marble in great temples built to honor them. Audiences of thousands gathered in vast open-air theaters with tiered seats arranged in a semicircle to watch actors perform scenes from myths and legends.

The *Iliad* and the *Odyssey*

These two epic poems were written down in the 8th or 7th century BCE and attributed to the Greek writer Homer. However, the tales were probably known to people centuries earlier and passed on by word of mouth. The first poem, the *Iliad*, tells the story of the Greek war against Troy, a city on the west coast of Turkey. The *Odyssey* describes the adventures of the hero Odysseus as he sails across the Mediterranean while returning from Troy to his home on the Greek island of Ithaka—a journey that takes 10 years!

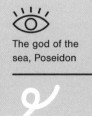
The god of the sea, Poseidon

The king of the gods, Zeus

Gods and Goddesses

The Greeks worshiped many gods, whom they believed lived on Mount Olympus. They made offerings to them and held festivals, plays, and sports competitions in their honor. In return, they believed that the gods would protect them. They traveled to the Oracle at Delphi to ask the gods to predict the future and advise on political matters.

Zeus was the king of the gods and Hera his queen. Other deities included Aphrodite (goddess of love), Apollo (god of music and prophecy), and his twin sister, Artemis (goddess of hunting and childbirth). There were also the powerful Poseidon (god of the sea) and Hades (god of the underworld). Athena, goddess of wisdom and war, had a special role as protector of the city of Athens. In art, each god or goddess could be identified by what they were carrying—for example, Poseidon carried a trident and Apollo a stringed instrument called a *kithara*.

Terracotta Lekythos (oil flask)

Greek, ca. 460–450 BCE

Apollo is pictured holding an instrument called a kithara. According to legend, he was born under a date palm tree, which is also featured on the flask.

Terracotta Amphora (Jar)
Greek, ca. 540–530 BCE

Hercules, featured on many pieces of pottery, was a strong and brave hero. He was the son of Zeus, so was part god, part mortal. Here, Hercules aims an arrow as he completes one of the 12 tasks he was challenged to perform by King Eurystheus.

Marble Statue of a Wounded Amazon
Roman, 1st–2nd century CE

Terracotta Lekythos (Oil Flask)
Greek, ca. 500 BCE

In this scene from the *Iliad*, the sea nymph Thetis (mother of the Greek hero Achilles) is pictured in a chariot drawn by winged horses. Deities Iris and Hermes are traveling with her.

Terracotta Amphora (Jar)
Greek, ca. 530 BCE

On this jar, we see Hercules wrestling the god Apollo for control of a peculiar-looking object. This is the Delphic tripod, the sacred seat of the Oracle of Delphi.

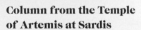

Terracotta Volute-Krater (Bowl for Mixing Wine and Water)
Greek, ca. 450 BCE

Greek artists rarely painted actual historical battles, like their victory in the Persian Wars. Instead, they pictured clashes from myths and legends. This large bowl for mixing wine and water shows a number of famous fights. Along the top, there is a battle between Greeks and centaurs (half man, half horse); below, is a contest between the Greeks and the Amazons, a mythical race of female warriors.

Column from the Temple of Artemis at Sardis
Greek, ca. 300 BCE

This fragment of a vast marble column is from a temple dedicated to the goddess Artemis that once stood in the city of Sardis (in modern-day Turkey). This pillar is topped with two scroll-like spirals—a characteristic feature of the Ionic order.

Group of 15 Terracotta Comic Actors
Greek, late 5th–early 4th century BCE

Greeks would have recognized the different roles these clay actors are playing by their poses, costumes, and masks. In Greek theater, all parts were played by men. These figures were originally painted and may have been made as souvenirs.

Ancient Rome

Legend tells that Rome was founded in 753 BCE by brothers Romulus and Remus. For centuries, Rome was a republic ruled by a senate of citizens; the powerful Roman army fought wars in Italy and beyond, adding more and more land to their territory. The first leader to be declared emperor in 27 BCE was Augustus, the adopted son of Julius Caesar. At its peak, the Roman Empire stretched from Egypt to as far north as Scotland. Across the empire are the remains of Roman roads, buildings, thermal baths, mosaic floors, and sculptures.

Did you know?

Wealthy Romans were born citizens and enjoyed special privileges. It was possible to become a citizen another way—by fighting in the army or navy. This bronze diploma granting citizenship was awarded after 25 years of service in the Roman navy.

Portrait Heads

The Romans were famous for their portrait heads. Unlike the Greeks, who enjoyed beautiful, ideal forms, Roman aristocrats and emperors were often pictured "warts and all," with messy hair, stubble, or a frown.

Bronze Military Diploma Fragment
Roman, 113–114 CE

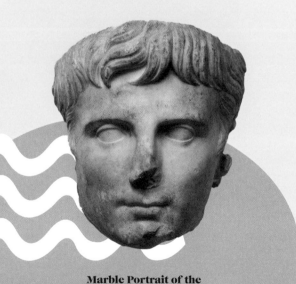

Marble Portrait of the Emperor Augustus
Roman, ca. 14–37 CE

Many sculptures were made of the emperor Augustus, who died at the age of 77. But in all of them, he is shown as a young man.

Marble Portrait of the Emperor Constantine I
Roman, ca. 325–70 CE
Constantine's huge marble head is almost 3 ft (1 m) tall. It would have been attached to an even bigger body.

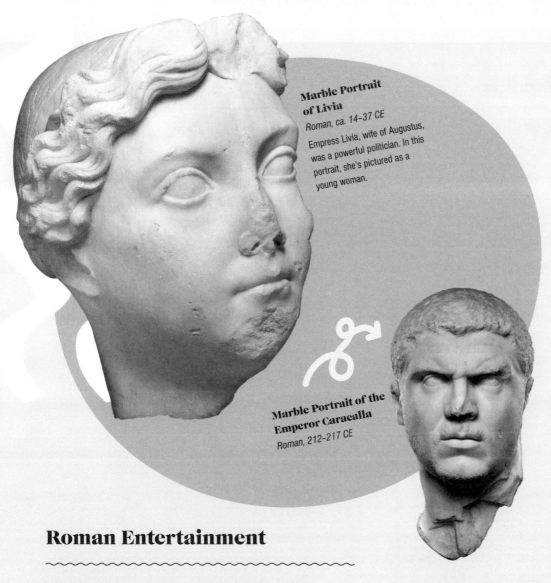

Marble Portrait of Livia
Roman, ca. 14–37 CE
Empress Livia, wife of Augustus, was a powerful politician. In this portrait, she's pictured as a young woman.

Marble Portrait of the Emperor Caracalla
Roman, 212–217 CE

Gold Aureus of Julius Caesar
Roman, 46 BCE

Gold Aureus of Augustus
Roman, 20–19 BCE

Roman Entertainment

Gladiator battles were popular across the Roman world. According to the historian Livy, the earliest gladiatorial contest was in 264 BCE, during the First Punic War. The Colosseum in Rome was built in the 70s CE and dedicated in 80 CE to stage lavish, spectacular fights in front of a vast crowd, in the presence of the emperor. Gladiator schools trained different types of fighters, who were each dressed and armed in a particular way. Many were prisoners or slaves.

Terracotta Statuette of a Gladiator
Roman, 1st–2nd century CE
Dressed in protective body armor, this gladiator carries a shield and short sword.

Carnelian Intaglio of a Gladiator Fighting a Lion
Roman, 1st half of 1st century CE
Carnelian, a hard red-orange stone, was engraved to make rings and seals. When pressed into hot wax, the picture appeared in 3D.

Gold Aureus of Octavian
Roman, 39 BCE

Making Art

Artists working in ancient Rome created pieces for high-ranking wealthy families. Romans copied Greek sculptures and placed them in their homes and villas. They commissioned portraits of themselves, dressed in fine clothes, and wore elaborate jewelry.

Marble Head of an Athlete
Roman, ca. 138–192 CE

Statues

Statues of Roman leaders were put in public places. Many sculptures created in bronze have since been melted down; marble ones, though often broken into fragments, have survived.

Bronze Statue of an Aristocratic Boy
Roman, 27 BCE–14 CE

An artisan making a sculpture with a chisel and mallet

Marble Bust of a Woman
Roman, mid-3rd century CE

Marble Bust of a Man
Roman, mid-1st century CE

Carnelian Ring Stone

Roman, ca. 1st–3rd century CE

Here, an artist is adding the finishing touches to a marble bust. He's probably holding a paintbrush—Roman sculptures were often brightly painted.

Sardonyx Cameo Portrait of the Emperor Augustus

Roman, ca. 41–54 CE

Here, the artist has created a two-colored portrait by carving into sardonyx, a gem that has different colored layers of stone. Augustus is depicted as a god, wearing a cape and a head decoration.

Precious Stones

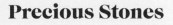

Carving precious stones became very popular in Roman times. Gems like orange carnelian were cut with elaborate designs; artists either carved shapes into the stone (intaglio) or cut away, leaving a design in relief (cameo). Carved gems were often set into rings and used as seals.

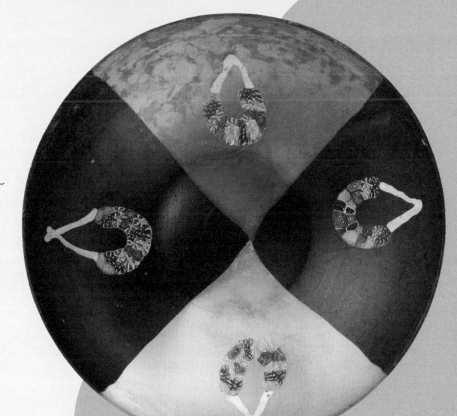

Glass Garland Bowl

Roman, late 1st century BCE

This bowl was crafted by joining four separate segments of colored glass. Each one is inlaid with a decorative glass pattern called *millefiori*, fashioned to look like a garland of flowers.

Brooch

Roman, 100–200 CE

Ornaments like this decorated silver brooch were set with precious stones and layers of gold.

Roman Homes

Wealthy Romans would have had both a town and a country residence. Country villas were places to retreat to outside the city in the hot summer months. They were often large, filled with fine courtyards, mosaic floors, and rooms decorated with fresco wall paintings. Well-tended gardens contained flowers, trees, fountains, and even sculptures.

Did you know?

The cities of Pompeii and Herculaneum were preserved when the volcano Vesuvius erupted in 79 CE. Whole regions, streets, buildings, artifacts, people, and pets were deeply buried under soot and ash and were preserved for 2,000 years, giving us a glimpse into everyday life in Roman Italy.

Cubiculum (Bedroom) from the Villa at Boscoreale
Roman, ca. 50–40 BCE

Mosaic Floors

Wealthy Roman homes included mosaic floors—intricate designs created with tiny stones in many colors called *tesserae*. This 2nd-century mosaic floor panel is from a home in Daphne, a popular country retreat near the city of Antioch, in modern-day Turkey. It shows a female figure wearing garlands of flowers and leaves; she represents Spring.

Fresco Depicting Townscapes from the Villa at Boscoreale
Roman, ca. 50–40 BCE

A Villa in Boscoreale

These frescoes were painted on the walls of a villa in Boscoreale on the Bay of Naples, close to Mount Vesuvius. At one point, the villa was owned by a man named Publius Fannius Synistor. The paintings show architecture and objects as if they are real. This illusion is typical of fresco painting in the 1st century BCE. The style is known as *trompe l'oeil*, meaning "trick (or deceive) the eye."

Fresco Showing a Bowl of Fruit from the Villa at Boscoreale
Roman, ca. 50–40 BCE
One of the walls in the villa features this painting of a bowl of fruit. Pictured in a glass bowl on a red "shelf," they look ready to be eaten!

Religious Beliefs

Like the Greeks, most Romans worshiped many gods. Across the Roman Empire, we can find shrines to gods in the home for personal worship and temples dedicated to particular deities, where offerings were made.

Christianity

The beginnings of Christianity were in the 1st century CE, at the height of the Roman era. Christians followed the teachings of Jesus, who was crucified in Jerusalem around 30–33 CE. Like those of the Jewish faith, Christians worshiped one god, rather than many. In 313 CE, Roman Emperor Constantine made Christian worship legal, and eventually the religion spread across the empire.

Gold Funerary Wreath
Roman, 1st–2nd century CE

Marble Sarcophagus with the Triumph of Dionysos and the Seasons
Roman, ca. 260–270 CE

Death and Burial

From around the 2nd century BCE, the Romans buried their dead rather than cremating them. The wealthiest Romans were buried in carved stone coffins known as *sarcophagi*. These were decorated with scenes from famous battles, myths, and legends or with figures representing the four seasons. Later, sarcophagi featured images of Christian saints.

Portrait of a Young Woman with a Gilded Wreath

Egypt (Roman period), 120-140 CE

The young woman in this lifelike portrait wears a golden wreath like the one pictured opposite. Portraits such as this one were painted on coffins found in Fayum, Egypt. They covered the faces of bodies that were mummified for burial according to Egyptian tradition. The portraits are painted on wood using encaustic—paint mixed with hot wax.

Marble Relief Fragment with the Head of Mars

Roman, early 3rd century CE

Bronze Statuette of Neptune

Roman, 2nd century CE

Roman Gods

Bronze Statuette of Minerva

Roman, 2nd century CE

Pluto, the god of the underworld, with his three-headed dog, Cerberus

Bronze Statuette of Jupiter Capitolinus

Roman, 1st-2nd century CE

Silver Statuette of Venus

Roman, 1st-2nd century CE

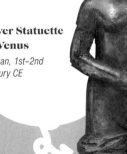

Arms and Armor

Over thousands of years, makers of arms and armor from many cultures across the world have fashioned objects that protect and adorn the head and body. Using the latest techniques of metalworking, leather working, and embroidery, their designs protected the wearer from injury when attacking and defending in combat. In parades and ceremonies, they made the wearers look impressive and inspiring.

Did you know?

Japanese Samurai warriors first appeared in historical records in the 10th century CE. The word *samurai* means "those who serve." They were known for intricate armor, and their helmets were fashioned into bold and striking designs.

Profile Warrior Ornament

Moche, South America, 6th–7th century

Sallet in the Shape of a Lion's Head

Italy, ca. 1475–80

Made of embossed and gilt copper fitted over steel, this finely crafted lion's head helmet connected its wearer to Hercules, the strong and courageous Greek hero who famously wore a lion's head and cloak in battle.

Helmet

Japan, 5th century

Don't Lose Your Head!

Helmets like these not only protected heads in combat but also provided a focus for some of the finest decoration and crafting of the time. Great leaders could be marked out and identified at all times by the fine decoration or special shape of the helmet they wore. Take a look at the hats and helmets on this page. They include a bronze Corinthian helmet, shaped to protect the wearer's face while allowing them to see and hear what's happening. The pointed turban helmets from Iran and Turkey are inscribed with religious writings from the Koran to protect the wearer. There's even an example of protective headgear for a horse, called a *shaffron*.

Turban Helmet

Turkey or Iran, 15th century

Tibetan War Mask

*Mongolia or Tibet,
12th–14th century*

Helmet

*Mesopotamia or Iran,
5th century*

Turban Helmet

Iran, 15th century

**Burgonet with
Falling Buffe**

France, ca. 1550

Bronze Helmet

*Crete, Greece, late 7th
century BCE*

**Shaffron
(Horse's Head Defense)**

*Tibet or Mongolia, late
15th–early 17th century*

Bascinet

*possibly France,
ca. 1375–1425*

Helmet

Turkey, ca. 1560

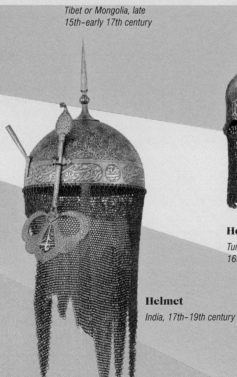

Helmet

India, 17th–19th century

Helmet with Aventail

*Turkey, late 15th–
16th century*

Visored Bascinet

Italy, 1425–1450

**Helmet
(Zukinnari Kabuto)**

Japan, 16th century

Armor for the Body

Like the head, the body must be protected! Warriors often rode into battle on horseback so horses often wore armor. Here, you can see everything from heavy articulated suits of armor, like the one made for King Henry VIII of England, to individual pieces that slotted onto different parts of the body, like the arm guard from India. Mail armor, like the mail shirt from Tibet, below, was made from fine metal links to stop blades cutting deeply through the body. The knotted leather torso armor of the Dali Kingdom in China, like the armor for the torso and hips pictured opposite, was coated with lacquer to form a protective shell.

Chess Piece
Western Europe, possibly England,
ca. 1350–1360

Armor (Gusoku)
Japan, 18th century

Did you know?

Chess, a game in which two opposing armies battle each other, was invented in India in the 6th century CE. Intricately carved chess sets designed in medieval Europe show warriors on horseback dressed for battle. The knight piece, left, and his horse wear mail armor and protective headgear of steel plates.

Mail Shirt
Tibet, possibly Bhutan or Nepal, 17th–19th century

Armor (*Yoroi*) of Ashikaga Takauji

Japan, 1305–1358

Fabric Armor and Helmet with Buddhist and Taoist symbols

Korean, possibly 18th century

Ceremonial Armor for a High Ranking Official

China, 18th century

Armor Garniture of George Clifford, Third Earl of Cumberland

Great Britain, 1586

Armor (*Gusoku*)

Japan, 16th and 18th centuries

Armor for the Torso and Hips

China, 12th–13th century

Arm Guard (*Dastana*)

India, 18th century

Defense for the Lower Right Leg (Greave)

Turkey, mid-15th century

Armor of Mail and Plate

India, late 18th–first half of the 19th century

Field Armor of King Henry VIII of England

Italy, ca. 1544

Shirt of Mail and Plate

Iran or Turkey, 15th–16th century

Weapons and Shields

Throughout history, fighters used a great variety of weapons to attack and shields to defend. Spears, swords, firearms, clubs, and javelins were made from metal and other materials worked into intricate shapes and decorated with images that were considered to have protective power. Some show scenes from myths and legends, family crests, coats of arms, initials or monograms, or religious words. Swords were also made for use in ceremonies where leaders were formally given their powers—like the jewel-encrusted saber with scabbard grip, designed for the investiture of the sultan.

Dagger with Scabbard
India, Mughal, 1605–1627

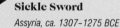

Sickle Sword
Assyria, ca. 1307–1275 BCE

Ax Head (Middle Kingdom—Early New Kingdom)
Egypt, ca. 1981–1550 BCE

Blade and Mounting for a Short Sword (*Wakizashi*)
Japan, blade 16th century; mounting 19th century

Bronze Shield Boss with Griffin and Sphinx Frieze
Etruscan, ca. 650 BCE

Shield for the Field or Tournament (*Targe*)
Germany, ca. 1450

Shield Boss (*Umbo*)
Western Europe, 7th century

Shield
Hunkpapa Lakota/Teton Sioux, Native American
ca. 1885

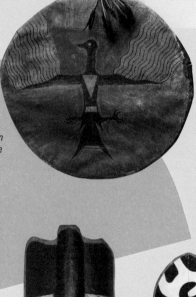

Archer's Shield (*Pavise*)
Switzerland, 15th century

Model Shield
Egypt, ca. 1981–1802 BCE

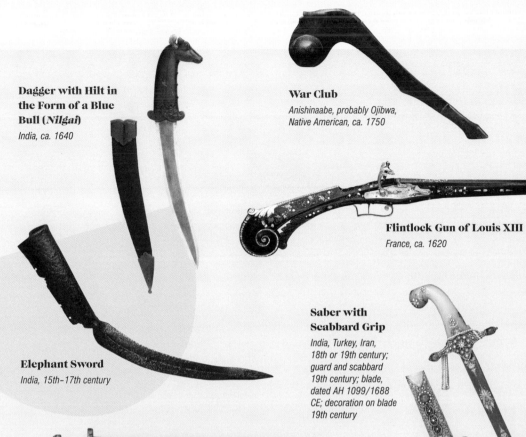

Dagger with Hilt in the Form of a Blue Bull (*Nilgai*)
India, ca. 1640

War Club
Anishinaabe, probably Ojibwa, Native American, ca. 1750

Flintlock Gun of Louis XIII
France, ca. 1620

Shields

Large shields offered a fine space for decoration. This one from Rajasthan in the north of India is made of lacquered leather, gold, and silver and is painted with animals, plants, and flowers. On the left of this page, the wooden shield of the Moro people of the Philippines is adorned with bold, geometric patterns.

Elephant Sword
India, 15th–17th century

Saber with Scabbard Grip
India, Turkey, Iran, 18th or 19th century; guard and scabbard 19th century; blade, dated AH 1099/1688 CE; decoration on blade 19th century

Viking Sword
Europe, probably Scandinavia, 10th century

Shield (*Dhàl*)
India, ca. 1800

Shield
Philippines, Moro 18th–19th century

Shield for the Field or Tournament (*Targe*)
Germany, ca. 1450–1500

Shield Depicting Saint George Slaying the Dragon
Italy, ca. 1560–1570

Shield of King Henry II of France
France, ca. 1555

Standing Shield
Germany, 1385–1387

Shield (*Adarga*)
Mexico, probably mid-18th century

Animals in Asian Art

Art makers across Asia were inspired by the animals that roamed its mountains, valleys, and farmlands. The objects pictured here are thousands of years old, the earliest being from civilizations that bloomed around 4,000 years ago in India and Pakistan's Indus valley and China's Yellow River and Yangtze valleys. On these pages, we can also see examples from Japan, Korea, Cambodia, Thailand, and Vietnam—a mix of pottery and terracotta pieces; objects carved in marble and jade; and elaborate vessels, ornaments, and pieces of jewelry cast in bronze or fashioned in gold.

Woman Riding Two Bulls
India, 2000–1750 BCE

This female figure, who may be a goddess, kneels on a platform that is supported by two powerful bulls. She's holding on to the humps on their backs.

Marble Tiger

China, 11th–9th century BCE

The tigers that roamed Asian forests can be found on many ancient ornaments and are symbols of power and bravery. This piece of patterned marble mimics the creature's distinctive markings. Three holes on the tiger's back suggest that the object was used to contain something, possibly cosmetics.

Ornament, Winged Feline

China, 4th–3rd century BCE

This fantastical winged creature combines parts of different animals. It strikes an elegant pose with its catlike claws and curved tail.

Bracelet with Dragonflies
Thailand, 300 BCE–200 CE

The delicate curved wings and bodies of two dragonflies decorate this fine bronze bracelet.

Ear Ornaments with Elephant & Winged Lion

India, ca. 1st century BCE

These finely crafted earrings are decorated with images of a lion and an elephant. They are fashioned from many pieces of hammered gold, adorned with tiny gold beads.

Incense Burner with Dragon Spout

Vietnam, 1st–3rd century

This elaborate bronze burner, with its long, sleek spout, takes the form of a winged dragon, in whose round belly the incense would be placed.

Eating and Drinking

Animal forms were found on many pots and vessels. Fine examples were used for serving and storing food and for special ceremonies and rituals.

Ewer with Elephant-Headed Spout

Vietnam, late 2nd–3rd century

This jug is cast in bronze. Its spout is finely crafted to resemble the head and trunk of an elephant.

Standing Ganesha

Cambodia, second half of the 7th century

Ganesha, an important Hindu deity, can be identified by his elephant head. By 700 CE, he was being worshiped in many parts of Southeast Asia, by Buddhists and Hindus alike.

Bird-Shaped Vessel

Korea, 3rd century

This rare vessel, discovered in a burial site, was probably used as part of funeral rituals. The opening on the bird's back can be filled with water, which is poured out through its tail.

Jade in China

The use of jade in China dates from around 5000 BCE. Ancient jades were made from the mineral nephrite, a stone harder than steel that was extracted from mountains and river beds. Jade carving required great technical skill. Until the invention of diamond tools, early jades were shaped by grinding with sand, a labor-intensive process that would have taken weeks or even months.

Knotted Dragon Pendant

China, 3rd century BCE

This pendant looks like coiled rope. At its tip, the artist has carved a dragon's head.

Water Buffalo

China, 13th–11th century BCE

Objects like this jade water buffalo, engraved with fine lines and decorative patterns, were worn as talismans to bring good luck.

Pig in Recumbent Position

China, 1st–2nd century

Pigs were symbols of wealth in ancient China. Objects like this one, found buried with its owner, were believed to bring good fortune in the afterlife.

Standing Deer

China, 11th–9th century BCE

This carved jade deer with delicate, curved horns and elegant hooves was worn as a pendant and may have been a talisman.

Precious Objects

Jade was believed to have powerful magical properties. Jade pieces were used in religious ceremonies and rituals. They were given as offerings to gods and ancestors, while carved objects and pendants were buried with the dead. Disk-shaped pieces known as Bi and tube-shaped Cong were found in tombs of important families.

Over time, objects lost their religious uses and instead showed the status of their owners. Jade objects were fashioned into ornaments, such as belt buckles, scabbard holders, and combs. From the 1st century CE, pure white jade was held in the highest regard.

Notched Disk

China, 2400–1900 BCE

Disk-shaped objects like this one, carved from a fine piece of jade and found in burial sites in Eastern China, are believed to represent heaven.

Comb

China, 25–220 CE

This comb is made of white jade and gold, decorated with a floral pattern.

Ritual Object

China, ca. 2400 BCE

The exact function of this dark jade, tube-shaped object is still a mystery to archaeologists. This one, and others like it, are believed to have had protective powers.

Ceremonies and Rituals in China

The bronze objects on this page were crafted in China more than 3,000 years ago. They were used in special ceremonies and rituals, designed to connect the world of the living with that of the dead. Gods and ancestors played an important role in society. People prayed to them, asking for advice and protection. They honored them with offerings of food and wine.

Upright Bell (*Nao*)

China, 13th century BCE

Bronze bells were produced in sets. They could produce two different notes, depending on where they were struck with a mallet. Like the cauldron to the bottom left of this page, this bell is decorated with the face of a mythical monster, known as a "taotie." The nao type of bell is not suspended but oriented upward with its stem set into a socketed base.

Ceremonial Objects

Incredible bronzes were created in China's Shang (ca. 1600–1046 BCE) and Zhou (1046–256 BCE) dynasties. Decorated cauldrons, pots, and buckets were used to hold food and wine (in some, traces still remain). They were buried with their owners so they could be used in the afterlife.

Rectangular Cauldron (*Fangding*)

China, 12th–11th century BCE

This cauldron depicts a "taotie," a masklike face of a mythical monster. It is shown with bulging eyes and curved horns.

Bell (*Niuzhong*)

China, early 5th century BCE

Decorated with serpents and dragons, this Zhou dynasty bell would have been part of a large set, hung on a wooden frame.

Altar Set
China, late 11th century BCE

This set of bronze vessels was found buried in a tomb of an aristocrat from the Zhou dynasty. Each object is finely decorated with detailed patterns, dragons, birds, and masks.

Lobed Tripod Cauldron (*Liding*)
China, 12th–11th century BCE

Derived from everyday pottery cooking pots, ritual bronze tripod vessels were used to cook and serve food offerings.

Bronze

Chinese bronze vessels were made using a method called piece-mold casting. First, the object was modeled in clay and left to harden. Next, soft clay was pressed against the object and removed in sections, creating the "piece molds." The original model was then shaved down to create a space between the model and the molds, where liquid bronze (a mix of copper, tin, and a little lead) could be poured in. With this process, bronze objects could be incredibly detailed. Finely modeled patterns and pictures on the surface often feature real and imaginary animals and intricate curved shapes that look like mouths, claws, tails, horns, and flames. If you look closely, it's sometimes possible to see where different molds have been joined together.

Wine Cup (*Zhi*)
China, 13th century BCE

This wine cup is decorated with the image of an owl. Owls also decorate the lid.

The Beginnings of Buddhist Art

Buddhism, the world's fourth-largest religion, began in India around the 5th century BCE. Within 500 years, Buddhist art and ideas had traveled across Central and Southeast Asia, influencing, and being influenced by, other traditions along the way.

Depicting the Buddha

Images of the Buddha vary from region to region. Although the sculptures of the Buddhas on these pages share some features and poses, like coiled hair, elongated earlobes, and outstretched hands, the sculptors have approached the faces, bodies, and the way their clothing drapes around them in very different ways.

Standing Buddha
Indonesia
7th–8th century

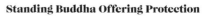

Standing Buddha Offering Protection
India, late 5th century

This red stone sculpture of the Buddha is full of symbolism. His halo shows the light of enlightenment streaming out from his body. He wears the robes of a monk that reveal his perfect form in a way that suggests yogic control as another important indication of his enlightenment.

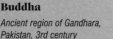

Buddha
Ancient region of Gandhara, Pakistan, 3rd century

Who was the Buddha?

Siddhartha Gautama, also known as Shakyamuni, Shaka, or the Buddha (meaning "enlightened one"), was born into a wealthy family in North India, around the 5th century BCE. Abandoning his riches at the age of 29, he embarked on a life of poverty and prayer, finding *bodhi*, or enlightenment, while meditating underneath a sacred fig tree. He decided to teach others how they, too, could follow this path.

Did you know?

In the ancient world, objects were transported and traded via many networks—by sea and on land. The Silk Road is the name given to a great network of routes, some of them treacherous, that connected the diverse regions within the Asian continent; the network also connected Asia with Africa and Europe. Precious objects, food, spices, and cloth were carried back and forth across the many routes; ideas, discoveries, and religion spread this way, too.

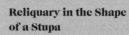

Reliquary in the Shape of a Stupa
Sri Lanka, 2nd–4th century

After the Buddha's death, his ashes were placed in pillared stone structures called *stupas*. Only fragments survive today. This relic container is designed to look like a *stupa*.

(Above) Birth of the Buddha Shakyamuni
Pakistan, ca. 2nd century

(Right) Buddha and Worshipers
Pakistan, 2nd–3rd century

These stone carvings from stupas in the ancient region of Gandhara, now Pakistan, contain scenes from the life of the Buddha. Buddhism arrived there from India around the 2nd century BCE, and the region was filled with many monasteries and *stupas*.

Two Lotuses, from the Bharhut Stupa
India, ca. 1st century BCE

Other motifs in Buddhist art include the wheel, a symbol of the cycle of life, and the lotus flower, which represents the Buddha's enlightenment.

Buddhism Across Asia

As Buddhism spread across Asia, the image of the Buddha changed from place to place. Over the centuries, the religion developed, too, and other deities were worshiped. In China, Japan, and Korea, a tradition known as Pure Land Buddhism focused on honoring the Buddha Amitabha and the Bodhisattva Avalokiteshvara. Followers of Pure Land believed that enlightenment could be found through faith and devotion.

China

Buddha, probably Amitabha
China, early 7th century

This seated Buddha from China is meditating, cross-legged. He is probably Amitabha, a celestial Buddha believed to preside over his Western Paradise or "pure land." He's made using the popular Chinese dry lacquer technique—a core, made of wood or clay, is covered with layers of cloth soaked in tree resin, which hardens like glue as it dries. His robe is painted with decorative patterns.

Bodhisattva, probably Avalokiteshvara (*Guanyin*)
China, ca. 550–560

Chinese sculptors often depicted bodhisattvas dressed in fine jewelry and clothing. Here, Avalokiteshvara wears an elaborate crown and fine pearl-and-bead necklaces.

Sri Lanka

Buddha Expounding the Dharma
Sri Lanka, late 8th century

The raised right hand of this Buddha from Sri Lanka shows that he is teaching.

Korea

Pensive Bodhisattva
Korea, 7th century

Here, Bodhisattva Maitreya sits in a thoughtful pose, with one leg crossed and a finger resting on his cheek. He is dressed in jewels and a crown.

Standing Buddha
Korea, 9th century

Thailand

Buddha Attended by Bodhisattvas Avalokiteshvara and Maitreya

Thailand, second half of the 8th century

This image shows the Buddha surrounded by two bodhisattvas. Avalokiteshvara (also known as Guanyin) is a compassionate deity who has remained in the world to help the faithful. Maitreya, who according to prophecy will one day be reborn as a Buddha, is often known as "Buddha of the future."

Four-Armed Avalokiteshvara, the Bodhisattva of Infinite Compassion

Thailand, 7th–8th century

Did you know?

Bodhisattvas are spiritual guides whose role is to teach others. Unlike the Buddha, they have not yet achieved enlightenment, although they may one day. The names and appearances of bodhisattvas vary from region to region.

Vietnam

Seated Buddha

Vietnam, 7th–8th century

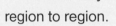

Indonesia

Standing Bodhisattva Maitreya or Manjushri

Indonesia, late 7th– early 9th century

Standing Buddha

Indonesia, 7th–8th century

Japan

The Bodhisattva Kannon (*Avalokiteshvara*)

Japan, mid-11th century

Kannon, one of the most popular bodhisattvas in Japanese Buddhism, is depicted here in flowing robes draped with sashes. This sculpture is carved from a single block of wood.

Central America, South America, and Mexico

From the high Andes mountains and desert plains of Peru to the thick jungles and rocky coasts of Mexico, the landscape varies dramatically. People began to settle in this vast region around 16,000 BCE, and they cultivated maize, squash, and beans and tapped rubber from the trees to make balls for sports. They wove cloth from cotton and the hair of llamas and alpacas. Through objects that have survived, we know about many of the region's early cultures.

House Model

Nayarit, 100 BCE–200 CE

People from what is now the state of Nayarit buried their dead with miniature sculptures of houses, temples, and even ball courts. These show scenes of people preparing food and feasting, perhaps in memory of the dead. They give us a great sense of life back then.

Mask

Olmec, 900–400 BCE

This Olmec mask is made from a hard green stone called jadeite and may show a ruler, a god, or powerful ancestor figure. It wasn't designed to be worn on the face. Holes pierced at the side indicate that it may have been worn around the body, as a necklace, on a belt, or attached to a buried body.

Mexico

The Olmec were based in the present-day states of Veracruz and Tabasco, on the east coast of Mexico. They ruled for 1,000 years, until 400 BCE, and are known for their colossal stone sculptures. The Olmec built Mesoamerica's first large cities and pyramids in La Venta and developed astronomy and a system of writing. Olmec cities were eventually abandoned, but some scholars believe that the Maya are descendants of the Olmec civilization. The Maya rose to prominence around 250 CE, and their influence spread as far south as Guatemala, Belize, Honduras, and El Salvador. Maya cities were even larger in scale than the Olmec sites and included temples, pyramids, plazas, and ball courts. Maya rulers, beliefs, and discoveries were documented in Maya script, which was carved in stone, painted on vessels, and written on paper.

Vessel

Maya, 7th–8th century

Deities of the ancient Americas included gods of the sun, moon, rain, crop production, and fertility. Chahk, pictured in profile on this cylindrical drinking cup, is the Maya rain god.

Ear Ornament, Winged Runner
Moche, 400–700 CE

This ear ornament, made from gold, colored stones, and shell, features a dramatic figure with the head of a bird.

Ornamental Plume
Pukara or early Tiwanaku, 200 BCE–400 CE

This finely hammered gold plume is decorated with designs featuring geometric patterns, birds, and a wide-eyed figure. It may have been used as a headdress ornament.

Border Fragment, Figures with Staves
Paracas, 4th–3rd century BCE

This colorful woven cloth was found in a tomb. Five figures holding staffs stare out, with large, circular eyes.

Drum
Nazca, 1st century

This ceramic drum was made in southern Peru. The drum skin would have been stretched over the flat, circular bottom of the figure. The eyes of the figure are also orca whales. Snakes coil around his head and crawl down his belly.

Peru

Peru, a country divided by the high Andes mountains that run from the north to the south, has been home to many different cultures. Today, they are known by the name of the place where they lived. These include Chavín (10th–5th century BCE), Paracas (800–100 BCE), Nazca (around 100 BCE–800 CE), and Moche (200–850 CE). Because of the dry conditions of the desert, some fragile objects—including brightly colored textiles—that would have perished in other places have survived buried in the ground for thousands of years.

The Sculpture of Mesoamerica

From the colossal stone heads of the Olmec to the relief sculptures that line the walls of Maya temples, the art of Mesoamerica is largely sculptural. Gods, kings, and scenes of everyday life were carved in stone or modeled in clay; they were often painted in bright colors.

Mesoamericans worshiped many gods. Deities often took the form of humans, animals, birds, or fantastical figures that combined them all. Many Mesoamerican traditions continue to this day.

Chocolate

The Maya produced a bitter drink by roasting and grinding cacao beans native to the Americas and mixing them with water. This drink, called Xocolatl, became the basis for modern chocolate, but it was very different from the sweet confection we know today. The Maya mixture was an everyday beverage but played a big role in rituals and medicine. Traces of cacao can be found on many ancient drinking vessels.

Seated Figure
Olmec, 12th-9th century BCE
The Olmec created many "baby" figures like this one, which is hollow and carved in white clay. Historians don't know whether they were deities or portraits or had some other function.

Pair of Figures
*Nayarit, Ixtlán del Río,
1st century BCE–2nd century CE*
These figures, with their thin limbs and stout torsos, are typical of the Nayarit's Ixtlán del Río style. The male figure wears a hat, shoulder cloth, and loincloth; he holds a drum in one hand and raised drumstick in the other. His companion wears a shoulder cloth and skirt, and one of her arms is draped around his shoulder. They both wear ornaments in their ears and nose.

Relief Sculpture

Mexico or Guatemala, 770s

This painted stone relief sculpture was carved by a sculptor named Chakalte'. It was placed above the entrance to a temple in La Pasadita, Guatemala. A ruler sits on a throne; he's being presented with an elaborate headdress.

Maya Bird Deity Figure

Maya, 3rd–6th century

This figure represents the Principal Bird Deity, one of the most significant gods of the early Maya pantheon. The god was thought to embody jade, the most precious material in the ancient Maya world. He was closely associated with the Maya kings. In fact, this work may depict the deity himself or a royal wearing a Principal Bird Deity mask.

A Mesoamerican pyramid

Maya Seated King

Maya, 4th century

This statue of a finely dressed, cross-legged Maya king is an incense burner. Ritual offerings of burned incense were made to ancestors and deities in special ceremonies.

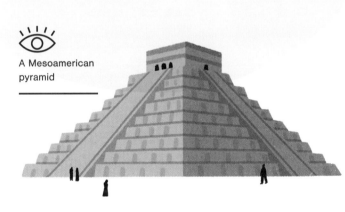

Earflare Frontals

Maya, 5th–7th century

As can be seen on many of the figures on this page, it was customary across many cultures in Mesoamerica to decorate the ears. These carved shell designs would have been set into a pair of ear ornaments.

Making Art

Some of the world's oldest and finest surviving textiles come from Peru, in the coastal region of Paracas. From their detail, we can tell that textiles were regarded very highly and held great importance. Sadly, cloth disintegrates easily and, compared to durable metal or clay objects, not many examples have survived. But the ones we do have (found buried in tombs in "mummy bundles" and preserved due to the region's hot, dry air) are today still brightly colored and show bold, intricate designs woven by skilled artisans.

Did you know?

The cloth used in many Peruvian garments was made from cotton and thread spun from the hair of animals of the Andes—the alpaca, llama, and vicuña.

Embroidered Mantle Fragment
Paracas, 5th–2nd century BCE

Mantle Fragment
Paracas, 5th–3rd century BCE

Border Fragment
Nazca, 2nd century BCE

Textile Making

Cloth was made by weaving, knotting, looping, and fringing thread and embroidering detailed patterns. Key patterns and motifs include flying or floating creatures, large-eyed faces, geometric shapes, and animals. Similar figures can also be found on pots and vessels from the period.

Bowls, Bottles, and Other Vessels

Peruvian vessels were often used as funerary offerings. They were carved and shaped into elaborate designs, and sometimes they displayed deities with animal features. After firing, some vessels were painted with a mix of mineral pigments and sticky plant resin.

Rattle Bowl with Oculate Being

Paracas, 3rd–1st century BCE

This bowl is painted with a flying or floating figure with a mix of animal and human features, typical of Paracas art. When heated, the resin becomes liquid and can be used as a binder. While cooling, the resin paint hardens and adheres to the ceramic vessel, creating a shiny surface.

Feline Bottle

Tembladera, Peru, 600–400 BCE

This bottle has a dramatically shaped spout that resembles a stirrup. Circular markings suggest the cat might be a jaguar or an ocelot.

Bottle with Caiman

Cupisnique, Peru, 1000–800 BCE

This bottle with beautifully preserved paint depicts the head of a caiman, or alligatorlike animal. The reptile's sharp teeth begin at the base of the long spout and wrap around the vessel, where one of the left handles forms its tongue. The right flange depicts a feline head, probably a jaguar. Both jaguars and caimans were thought to possess supernatural powers.

Cities

The great cities of Mesoamerica buzzed with life and were filled with fine palaces and art. The Olmec cities of San Lorenzo and La Venta, which flourished between 1150 and 400 BCE, were dominated by grand pyramids, now buried under grass mounds. Plazas were filled with colossal structures and giant heads, fashioned from stone brought from far away.

Teotihuacán

Mexico's Teotihuacán was one of the largest cities in the ancient world. By around 600 CE, between 100,000 and 200,000 people were living there. Its two towering pyramid structures—the Pyramid of the Sun and the Pyramid of the Moon—were connected by a long, straight road known as "The Street of the Dead." Walls were decorated with painted murals. The city was attacked and abandoned in 700 CE.

Mask
Teotihuacán, Mexico, 4th–8th century

Standing Figure
Teotihuacán, Mexico, 3rd–7th century

Yoke-Form Vessel
Maya artists, Teotihuacán, Mexico, mid-4th–mid-5th century

The Ball Game

In Mesoamerica, people played a number of different games with balls made from native rubber-producing plants. Though ball games had different rules over time and across Mesoamerican cultures, most had ritual significance and were played on rectangular ball courts at the ceremonial center of the city.

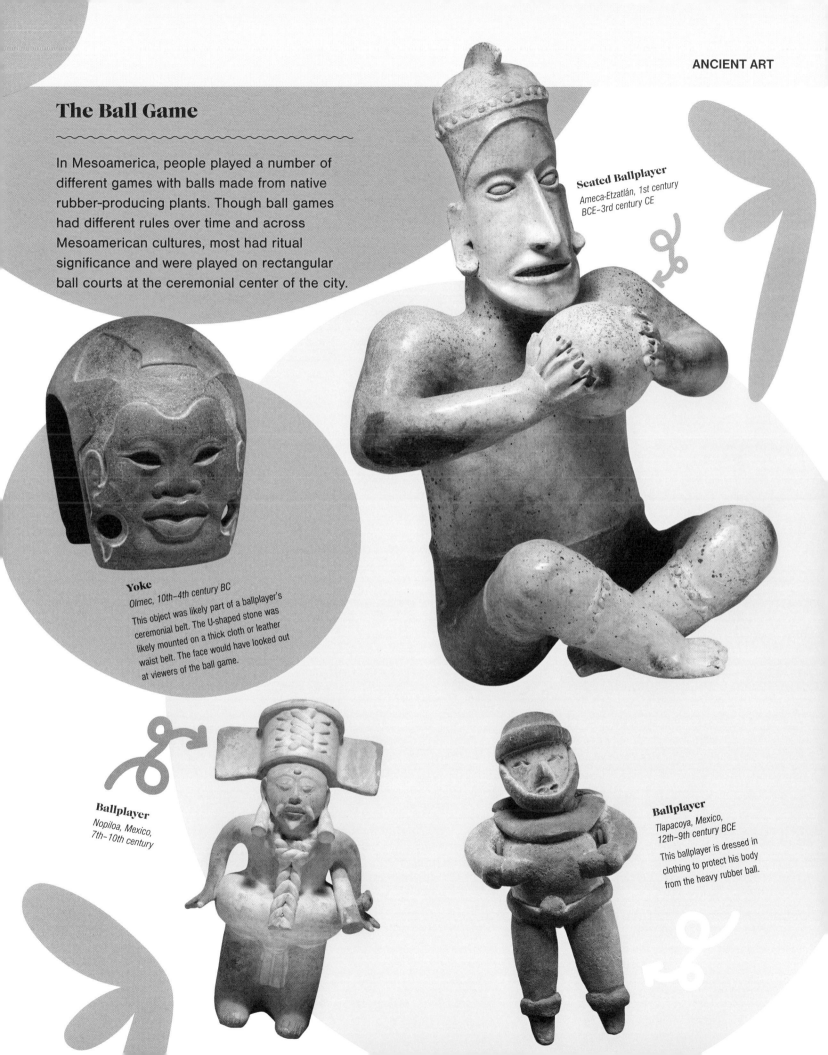

Seated Ballplayer
Ameca-Etzatlán, 1st century BCE–3rd century CE

Yoke
Olmec, 10th–4th century BC
This object was likely part of a ballplayer's ceremonial belt. The U-shaped stone was likely mounted on a thick cloth or leather waist belt. The face would have looked out at viewers of the ball game.

Ballplayer
Nopiloa, Mexico,
7th–10th century

Ballplayer
Tlapacoya, Mexico,
12th–9th century BCE
This ballplayer is dressed in clothing to protect his body from the heavy rubber ball.

2.

THE MEDIEVAL PERIOD

Islamic Art

The divine message was revealed to the Prophet Muhammad in Arabic in the early 7th century and later recorded and compiled into the Koran, Islam's holy book. Muslims believe that the Koran is the physical manifestation of God's message; therefore, the art of calligraphy became an exalted art form in Islamic art. Another characteristic of Islamic art is to cover whole surfaces with intertwined flowers, leaves, letters, and geometric shapes. Artists decorated buildings and objects of all kinds, both religious and secular.

Did you know?

In Islamic religious art, there are no images associated with God. Images of people and, to a certain extent, other creatures are usually discouraged in the sacred sphere but appear widely outside it. In the secular arts, figures are often shown in a stylized way.

Footed Cup
Iran, second half 14th century

This bronze cup, probably from Iran, dates from the Mongol period, when Mongol people conquered parts of the Muslim world. The cup's lotus flower motif became a common decoration during this time.

Standing Figure with Feathered Headdress
Iran, 12th–early 13th century

This life-size figure from the wall of a royal court probably felt like an extra person in the room! It might represent a ruler's guard, military chief, or other official.

Jar
Syria, 14th century

Islam's holy book, the Koran, was written in Arabic script. That's why calligraphy, or "beautiful writing," became an important art form. The tall white lettering on this jar wishes good fortune on the owner.

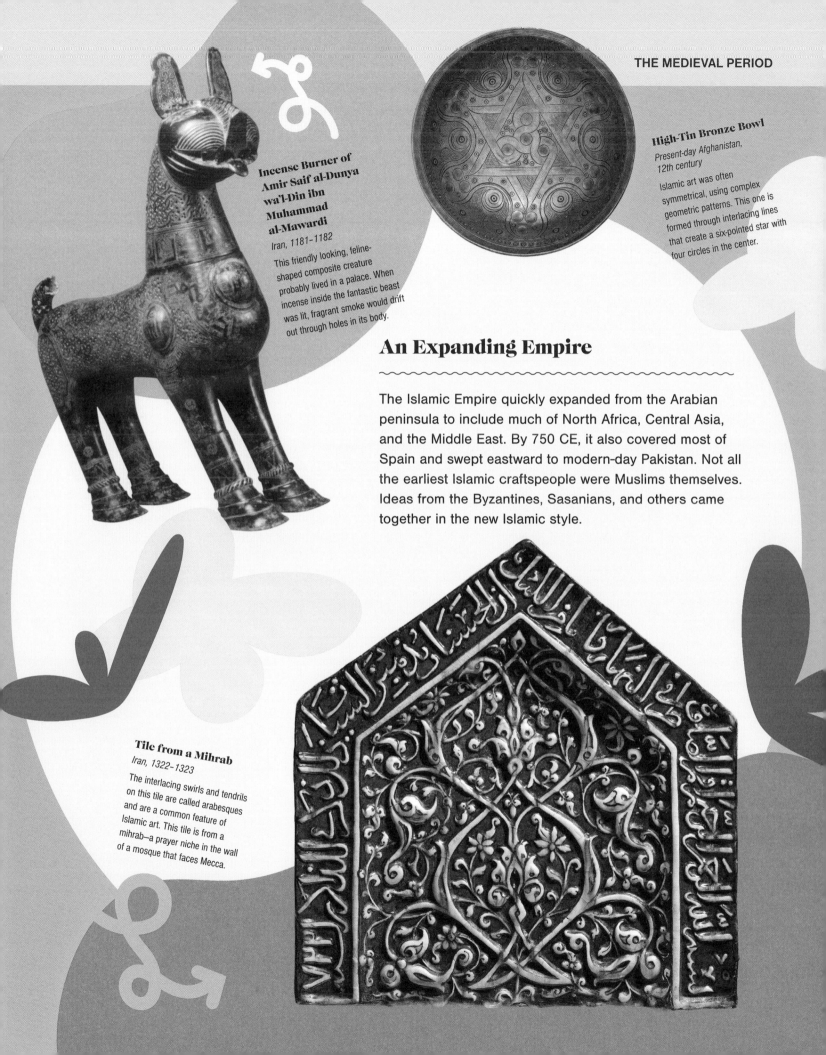

Incense Burner of Amir Saif al-Dunya wa'l-Din ibn Muhammad al-Mawardi
Iran, 1181–1182

This friendly looking, feline-shaped composite creature probably lived in a palace. When incense inside the fantastic beast was lit, fragrant smoke would drift out through holes in its body.

High-Tin Bronze Bowl
Present-day Afghanistan, 12th century

Islamic art was often symmetrical, using complex geometric patterns. This one is formed through interlacing lines that create a six-pointed star with four circles in the center.

An Expanding Empire

The Islamic Empire quickly expanded from the Arabian peninsula to include much of North Africa, Central Asia, and the Middle East. By 750 CE, it also covered most of Spain and swept eastward to modern-day Pakistan. Not all the earliest Islamic craftspeople were Muslims themselves. Ideas from the Byzantines, Sasanians, and others came together in the new Islamic style.

Tile from a Mihrab
Iran, 1322–1323

The interlacing swirls and tendrils on this tile are called arabesques and are a common feature of Islamic art. This tile is from a mihrab—a prayer niche in the wall of a mosque that faces Mecca.

A Place to Pray

As Islam grew, many mosques were built for people to gather and pray in. They varied in size and design but also had much in common. Inside, a niche called a mihrab marked the direction of Mecca. A minbar was a type of pulpit from which the Friday sermon and related speeches were delivered. Large mosques stood out against the skyline, with elegant domes and tall minarets from which voices rang out, calling the faithful to prayer.

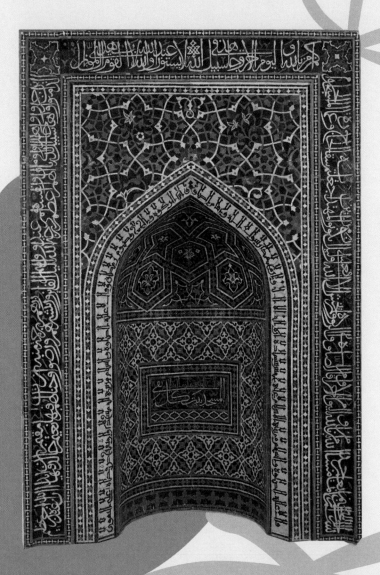

Mihrab (Prayer Niche)

Iran, 1354–55

The mihrab marks the direction of prayer and was an important feature in mosques and theological schools. Its arched shape was often shown on prayer mats.

Daily Worship

The Koran teaches that people should worship Allah five times a day. They can pray indoors or outdoors, as long as they face the direction of Mecca, Islam's holiest city.

Many people, however, pray in mosques. The first mosque was Muhammad's own house, made of mudbrick around a courtyard. Later, Islamic rulers had grand palaces with elaborate prayer rooms.

Mosques often include a dome and towers called minarets.

Pair of Minbar Doors

Egypt, ca. 1325–1330

To reach the minbar, the imam would walk through a pair of doors and climb some stairs. These minbar doors include intricate arabesques, carved in ivory and inlaid on wood.

"Laila and Majnun at School," Folio from a Khamsa (Quintet) of Nizami

Present-day Afghanistan, 1431–1432

This illustration shows a school for young children. A variety of books, including Korans, are part of the scene.

Mosque Lamp of Amir Qawsun

Egypt, ca. 1329–1335

Luxurious painted glass lamps like this one lit mosques, madrasas, monumental tombs, and other buildings. They were usually suspended from the ceiling on chains, giving off an atmospheric glow.

Ablutions Basin of Yemeni Sultan al-Mujahid Sayf al-Din 'Ali

Egypt or Syria, ca. 1321–1363

This basin was made for ritual washing before prayer—a requirement of Islam known as *wudu*. It belonged to a sultan, who is praised in the inscription engraved on it.

Studying Islam

Muslims were expected to study Islam's holy book, the Koran. Most *madrasas* (schools) were attached to mosques, and some included accommodations for students as well as classrooms and a prayer hall. Teaching focused on Islamic law as well as interpreting and memorizing the Koran. There were also separate schools for younger pupils.

The Art of Words

Writing, or calligraphy, was a highly esteemed art form in the Islamic world. The Arabic script revealed the words of Allah in the Koran, so it was deeply treasured. There were many styles of script, all suiting different purposes or signifying a certain place or period of time when they were produced. Some were simple, others swirling; some were long and low, others tall and stately. Calligraphy was practiced on paper, parchment, ceramics, textiles, wood, stone, and other materials. Sometimes, it gave a good luck message or the name of an object's owner.

Did you know?

In a proportional script, the letters that make up a word are carefully sized in relation to each other. The shape of each letter is determined by a set number of diamond-shaped dots, called rhombic dots. The diamond comes from the shape made by a calligrapher pressing their reed pen to the paper.

Folio from the "Blue Koran"

Tunisia, second half 9th–mid-10th century

A page from a Koran shows angular Kufic script. It is written in beautiful gold lettering on indigo-colored parchment.

Textile Fragment from the Dalmatic of San Valerius

Spain, 13th century

The fluid Naskh script was used for this inscription on a cleric's robe.

Varied Scripts

One of the earliest Islamic scripts was Kufic—a bold, angular style used in the first Koran. Another early script, Naskh, was more rounded and easier to read, so it became popular in everyday texts.

In the 10th century, six proportional scripts appeared, called the Six Pens. More scripts followed, all suited to different uses. For example, royal documents used complex scripts that were hard to forge.

Pen Box

Iran, late 13th–early 14th century

Calligraphy was very important, so related objects were often ornate. Imagine using this delicate pen box, decorated with silver and gold!

Inkwell with Zodiac Signs

Iran, early 13th century

Calligraphy with letters transforming into people or animals usually appears on metalwork objects, like this inkwell. Letters on its lid are sprouting human heads.

Talismanic Shirt

Attributed to Northern India or Deccan, 15th–early 16th century

Some inscriptions were made for good luck and protection, including on battle clothing. This shirt, worn under armor, goes one better. It displays the full Koran!

Bowl with Arabic Inscription

Iran, 10th century

A tall, "new-style" version of Kufic script spells out a proverb on this glazed bowl.

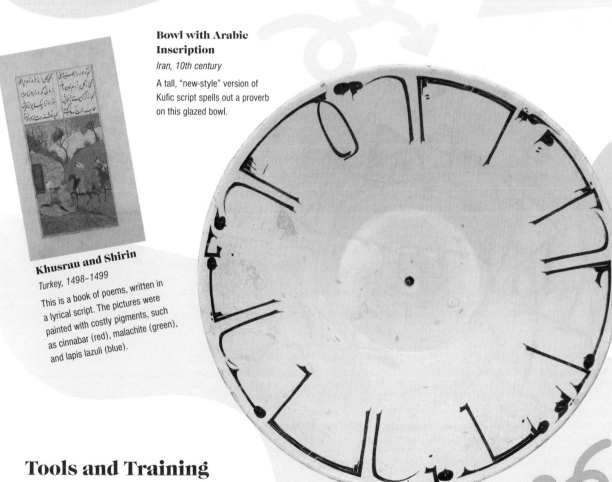

Khusrau and Shirin

Turkey, 1498–1499

This is a book of poems, written in a lyrical script. The pictures were painted with costly pigments, such as cinnabar (red), malachite (green), and lapis lazuli (blue).

Helmet with Aventail

Turkish, late 15th–16th century

This Turkish helmet is inscribed with names of warrior heroes. The aventail is the mail neck protector.

Tools and Training

Calligraphers were respected artists and usually highly educated people. They underwent specialized training for many years, learning by copying scripts. Some Muslim rulers became skilled calligraphers by studying with masters in the royal court. Most calligraphy was done by men, but a few women at court practiced it, too.

Calligraphers were taught how to prepare their own tools, such as pens made from hollow reeds. Writing was done on parchment or paper, which was introduced from China to the Islamic world in the 8th century.

Bifolium from a Koran

Turkey or Central Asia, ca. 14th century

Copying passages of text from the Koran was an act of devotion. Below is a bifolium—a double-page spread—in the Muhaqqaq script, a majestic proportional style.

The Art of Science

The period between the 8th and 14th centuries became known as the Islamic Golden Age. It was a time of great power and discovery, when science and other learning flourished. Islamic scholars translated ancient texts and developed new ideas and devices. Craftspeople created beautiful objects, from intricate instruments to complex patterns.

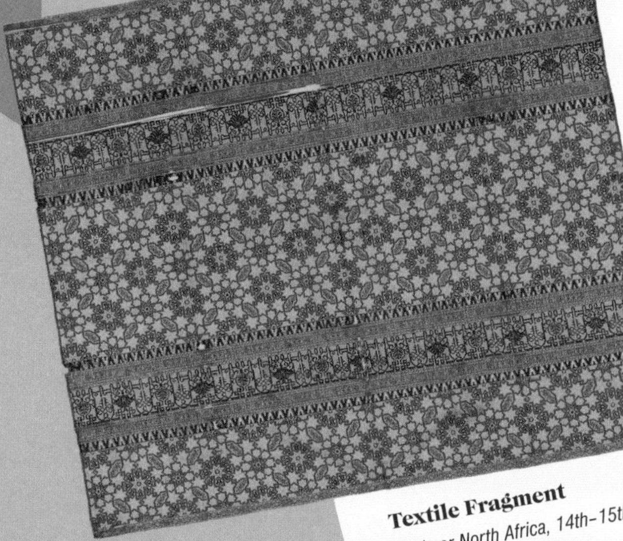

The Beauty of Geometry

Mathematicians and artists turned theories into breathtaking images. A system called tessellation helped them repeat shapes without any gaps. Patterns always started with a regular grid, to which more and more detail could be added. The two key tools were a compass and ruler, with designs based on circles and straight lines.

Textile Fragment

Spain or North Africa, 14th–15th century

This textile fragment illustrates how patterns could be repeated almost endlessly, using a grid.

Panel Made of Tiles

Iran, 1260–1270

Interlocking patterns, or tessellations, were well suited to ceramic tiling. These eight-point stars are tessellated with crosses, a popular pattern in Islamic art.

Science in the Stars

Since ancient times, people had used the stars to tell the time, predict the weather, and find their way around. Islamic scientists built on this knowledge to develop accurate clocks and other instruments. They used astronomy to determine when to pray and the direction of Mecca.

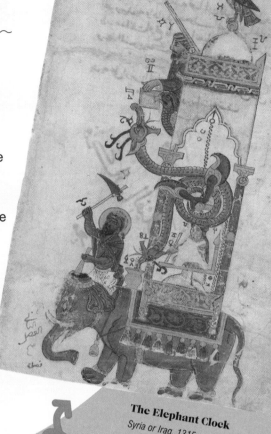

The Elephant Clock
Syria or Iraq, 1315

Believe it or not, this image from a *Book of the Knowledge of Ingenious Mechanical Devices* by al-Jazari is a design for a clock. Every half hour, the driver struck his mallet, the bird on top whistled, and a ball dropped into the dragon's mouth and then into a pot that clanged a gong!

Bowl with Courtly and Astrological Motifs
Iran, late 12th–early 13th century

Medieval astrologers identified seven "planets," visible to the naked eye. They are represented by the circular symbols on this bowl.

Preparing Medicine from Honey
Iraq, 1224

This Arabic translation of an ancient Greek text shows us what a medieval Islamic pharmacy might have looked like. The doctor is making medicine from honey to treat weakness and loss of appetite.

Health and Healing

Islamic physicians made great advances in understanding and healing the human body. They gathered old and new knowledge into libraries of books and authored a *Comprehensive Book of Medicine*. They developed natural medicines and pioneered original theories, such as how the human eye works. Many of their discoveries spread throughout the world and are still in use today.

1

Tiles

Ceramic tiles were first made in family workshops and became a huge industry in the Islamic world. There were various techniques for decorating tiles, including sparkly luster painting and colored glazes.

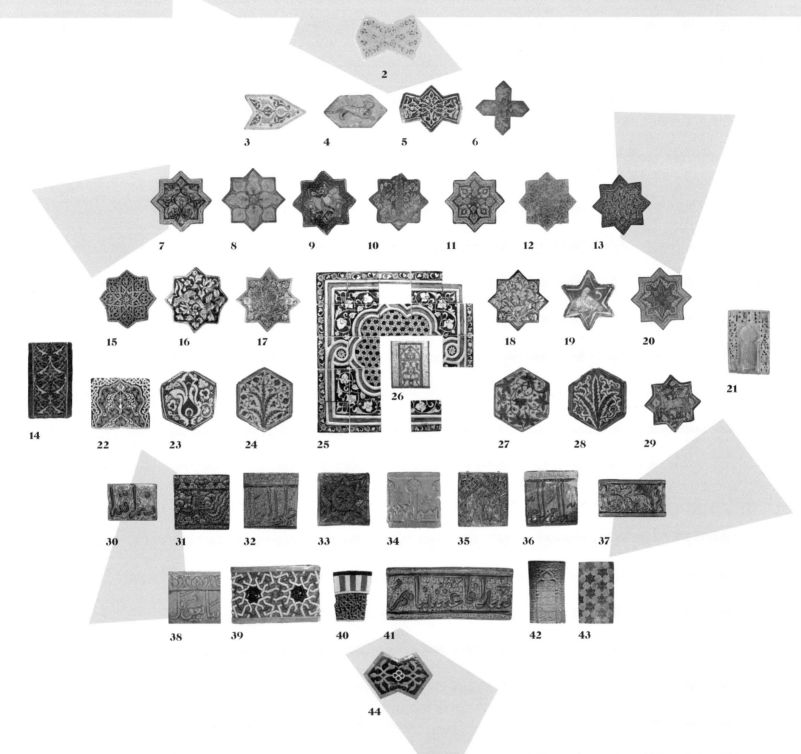

1. Hexagonal Tile Ensemble with Sphinx, ca. 1160s–1170s 2. Double-Pentagon-Shaped Tile, mid-13th–14th century 3. Tile, late 12th–early 13th century 4. Hexagonal Tile, early 13th century 5. Tile, 13th century 6. Cross-Shaped Tile, second half 13th century 7. Eight-Pointed Star Tile Depicting Animals and Inscription, dated AH 665/1267 CE 8. Star-Shaped Tile, 13th–14th century 9. Star-Shaped Tile, ca. 1300 10. Star-Shaped Tile, second half 13th century 11. Star-Shaped Tile, dated AH 663/1265 CE 12. Star-Shaped Tile, first half 15th century 13. Star-Shaped Tile, 14th century 14. Tile, AH 824/1421 CE 15. Carved Star Tile, early 13th century 16. Star-Shaped Tile, first half 14th century 17. Star-Shaped Tile, second half 13th–14th century 18. Tile, early 14th century 19. Star-Shaped Tile, 13th century 20. Star-Shaped Tile, 13th century 21. Tile with Niche Design, 12th century 22. Shaped Tiles in the "Cuerda Seca" Technique, late 14th century 23. Hexagonal Tile, first half 15th century 24. Hexagonal Tile, 15th century 25. Tile Panel, ca. 1430 26. Tile with Niche Design, dated AH 860/1455–1456 CE 27. Hexagonal Tile, 15th century 28. Hexagonal Tile, 15th–16th century 29. Star-Shaped Tile, 13th century 30. Tile from a Frieze, early 14th century 31. Tile with Image of Phoenix, late 13th century 32. Tile from an Inscriptional Frieze, early 14th century 33. Green Tile with Star Design, 12th–13th century 34. Tile from a Frieze, first half 13th century 35. Tile with Niche Design and Inscription, early 14th century 36. Tile from a Frieze, second half 13th century 37. Tile, 13th century 38. Tile from a Frieze, 13th century 39. Tile Decorated with Entrelacs Pattern Based on Octagons, second half 14th century 40. Architectural Tile with Partial Inscription, second half 14th century 41. Tile from a Frieze, late 13th century 42. Tile with Niche Design, dated AH 712/1312–1313 CE 43. Tile Panel, late 13th–14th century 44. Double Pentagon Shaped Tile, 15th century

The Byzantine Empire

In 330 CE, the Roman Emperor Constantine moved his capital city from Rome to Byzantion. He renamed it Constantinople (modern-day Istanbul) and declared Christianity the official religion of the empire. A new era of art began.

The first Christian churches were designed to inspire wonder. Churches were understood to represent Heaven on Earth, and gold was used to suggest a heavenly glow. Images were stylized, using lines and flat shapes. The idea was to represent the world as mysterious and spiritual.

John the Theologian and Prochoros
Byzantine, 15th century

In Byzantine art, gold was associated with the light of God. Fine sheets of gold leaf in the background of this painting suggest a divine setting.

Plate with the Battle of David and Goliath
Byzantine, 629–630

This silver plate, made in a palace workshop, was designed for display, not for dinner! It shows the biblical story of David and Goliath, with the figures wearing the dress of the early Byzantine court.

Boxes like this one were made to contain religious relics.

The Fieschi Morgan Staurotheke
Byzantine, early 9th century

The intricate art of cloisonné enamel work was perfected by the Byzantines. It meant twisting gold strips into tiny shapes and filling them with colored glass paste.

Solidus of Justinian II

Byzantine, 692–695

The Byzantines spoke Greek, but their coins were sometimes inscribed in Latin—a legacy from the western Roman Empire. The two sides of this gold solidus show Christ and the emperor, affirming who held power across the land.

The Hagia Sophia

Ages of Empire

Constantine ruled the Roman Empire, but after his death, it was split between East and West. The West, centered in Rome, collapsed in 476, but the East—the Byzantine side—held strong. It gained territory under Justinian I (527–565), who won back many former Roman lands. He also invested in great building projects in Constantinople and beyond.

In 634, the Byzantine Empire began to lose ground to Muslim armies from the Arabian Peninsula. Nevertheless, a new golden age began in the late 10th century. Trade flourished, with luxury items, precious metals, foods, and fabrics changing hands. The empire finally fell in 1453, when Turkish Muslims called the Ottomans invaded.

Capital with a Pattern of Leaves and Vines

Byzantine, 6th–7th century

Finely carved vines and leaves mask the density of stone in this column top, or capital. Patterns like this were popular in Byzantine churches, including the Hagia Sophia.

The Hagia Sophia

The creative triumph of Justinian I's reign was the Hagia Sophia. Built where two former churches had once stood, this one was bigger and more majestic. A massive dome, 108 ft (33 m) across, was held up by innovative engineering. Forty windows circled its base, giving the impression that the dome was floating above the building. Sparkling mosaics bounced light all around, seeming to dissolve the stone. Huge supporting columns were topped with carvings that looked like delicate lace. The Hagia Sophia took 10,000 laborers less than six years to build. Finished in 537, it was the world's biggest church for nearly 1,000 years.

Hanging Lamp in the Form of a Sandaled Right Foot

Byzantine, 5th century

Early Christians adopted the foot as a symbol of health and healing. This one served as a hanging lamp, lit by a wick that poked out of the big toe.

Icons

The Byzantine people had great faith in icons, which are images of holy figures, such as Christ and the saints. Icons are used as a way to talk directly with heavenly beings, to offer prayers and seek protection. They were bowed to, were kissed, and had incense and tapers lit before them. Armies would carry them into battle, and sailors took them out to sea. They ranged from the minuscule to the monumental, from necklace pendants to wall mosaics. Small wooden panel paintings were some of the most popular, especially for private devotion.

Halo from an Icon Cover

Byzantine, 10th–early 11th century

Many icons had protective covers, made of decorated metal. Windows in the cover revealed the icon beneath—a face under this halo, for example.

Icon with the Virgin and Child

Byzantine, mid-10th–mid-11th century

By the 1100s, the best-known icon image was the Virgin Hodegetria. She was shown cradling baby Jesus in her left arm while pointing to him with her right hand. According to legend, the original icon was painted by Saint Luke, from life. Every week, it was carried around Constantinople.

Triptych with the Mandylion
The Kremlin Armory Workshops, Moscow, 1637

Made by a Miracle

Some icons were known as *acheiropoieta*, meaning "made without hands." They were thought to have been created by a miracle and have special protective powers. One of the most famous was the Mandylion, a cloth imprinted with the face of Christ. This image was miraculously transferred to a tile called the Keramion, which became an acheiropoieton too.

Four Icons from a Pair of Doors (Panels), Possibly Part of a Polyptych: John the Theologian and Prochoros, the Baptism (Epiphany), Harrowing of Hell (Anastasis), and Saint Nicholas

Byzantine, early 15th century

Early Byzantine panel painters mixed their color pigments with hot wax. Later this was replaced with egg-based tempera paint, as used in these highly detailed door panels.

Iconoclasm

For a period of about 100 years, icons were banned in the Byzantine Empire. This was known as Iconoclasm, and it lasted from 726–787 and 815–843. Rulers believed it was wrong for people to worship images in place of the holy figures themselves. Icons were destroyed or plastered over, and very few that existed then survive today.

Wall Painting of Male Saint

Byzantine, 12th century, modern restoration

Larger icons, usually displayed in public places, included wall paintings on plaster, called frescoes. The pointed beard, sunken cheeks, and high forehead shown here suggest it is Saint John Chrysostom, a former archbishop of Constantinople.

Double-Sided Pendant Icon with the Virgin and Christ Pantokrator

Byzantine, ca. 1100

Christ Pantokrator, or Ruler of All, was a much-loved icon subject. With one hand holding a Gospel and the other raised in blessing, he gave confidence to the wearer of this enameled pendant.

Medallion with the Virgin from an Icon Frame

Byzantine, ca. 1100

This medallion in cloisonné enamel once formed part of an icon frame. A total of 12 discs, showing the Virgin, Christ, and the saints, surrounded a larger image of the archangel Gabriel.

Icon with the Crucifixion

Byzantine, mid-10th century

Some icons offered narrative scenes instead of individual figures. This ivory panel showing the Crucifixion was small enough to hold in the hand during private prayer.

Mighty Mosaics

The Roman tradition of mosaic making was not lost when the empire divided. In fact, the Byzantines took the art to an even more dazzling level! Most ancient mosaics were meant to be walked on and so used hard-wearing stone, but Byzantine versions mainly covered walls and ceilings and involved more fragile materials. Churches sparkled with images crafted from glass, gems, and gold and silver leaf. Mosaics also adorned palaces and state buildings, as well as smaller items. The Met is home to a number of modern replicas of medieval mosaics, as well as some originals.

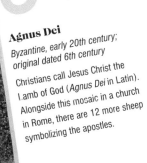

Agnus Dei
Byzantine, early 20th century; original dated 6th century
Christians call Jesus Christ the Lamb of God (*Agnus Dei* in Latin). Alongside this mosaic in a church in Rome, there are 12 more sheep symbolizing the apostles.

Emperor Justinian and Members of His Court
Byzantine, early 20th century; original dated 6th century
Some mosaics broadcast the authority of an emperor as well as the power of the Church. In this replica of a 6th-century mosaic, we see a haloed Justinian I, alongside soldiers, statesmen, and members of the clergy.

Sparkling Smalti

A Byzantine mosaic really came to life as light danced across its pieces, or tesserae. The Byzantines invented *smalti*—tesserae made of glass mixed with minerals to create a myriad of colors. The smalti contained air bubbles and were unevenly shaped, so they glinted in exciting ways. The other secret was gold leaf, which could be applied to clear glass, acting like a mirror. Tilting the smalti at different angles helped enhance their shine—for example, the mirror side might be tipped toward the viewer or toward a window to reflect the sunlight.

Display and Destruction

Mosaics on the walls and domes of early churches represented Christian religious figures. But during Iconoclasm, many religious mosaics were destroyed. Further damage happened during armed conflicts—including the Ottoman conquest of Constantinople (1453). At this point, the Hagia Sophia was converted into a mosque, and its mosaics were plastered over. They survived for hundreds of years before being uncovered and restored in the 19th and 20th centuries.

Archangel Gabriel

Byzantine, early 20th century; original dated 9th century

This is a replica of a mosaic from the 9th century. Notice how much detail went into a face, usually created from natural stone instead of glass. The brow, nose, and cheekbones are all given shape by wavy lines and subtle shifts of color.

Mother of God and Child

Byzantine, early 20th century; original dated 9th century

This is a replica of the oldest surviving mosaic in the Hagia Sophia. The original was made in the years after Iconoclasm. The ornately detailed figures are more than 13 ft (4 m) tall and seem to float in a sky of celestial gold.

Byzantine Luxury

2
Silver
The Attarouthi Treasure, Silver Dove
Byzantine, 500-650

A dove, representing the Holy Spirit, was often suspended above a church altar.

3
Enamel
Temple Pendant
Byzantine, ca. 1080-1150

This temple pendant hung near the forehead or cheek and had a perfumed cloth tucked inside.

4
Ivory
Casket with Warriors and Dancers
Byzantine, 11th century

Caskets (small boxes) like this one may have held scent bottles or jewelry in a wealthy Byzantine home.

1
Gold
Helmet (*Spangenhelm*)
Byzantine, 6th century

The decoration on this luxurious gilded helmet includes Christian symbols to protect the wearer.

5
Jewelry
Pendant Brooch with Cameo of Enthroned Virgin and Child and Christ Pantokrator
Byzantine, cameo late 1000s-1100s; mount 1100s-1300s

Luxury items poured out of Byzantine workshops, destined for wealthy owners. Constantinople was ideally located for trade in precious materials, such as gemstones from Asia and ivories from Africa.

6. Jeweled Bracelet (one of a pair), 500–700 **7.** Gold Necklace with Ornaments, 6th century **8.** Gold Necklace with Pearls and Stones of Emerald Plasma, 6th-7th century **9.** Necklace with Pendant Crosses, 6th-7th century **10.** Finger Ring, 5th-6th century **11.** Finger Ring, 10th century **12.** Solidus of Heraclius, Heraclius Constantine, and Heraclonas, 638–641 **13.** Basket Earring 10th-11th century **14.** Gold Bracelet, ca. 650 **15.** Gold Goblet with Personifications of Cyprus, Rome, Constantinople, and Alexandria, 8th century **16.** Bracelet with Grapevine Pattern, late 6th-early 7th century **17.** Earring, 6th-7th century **18.** Gold Signet Ring with Virgin and Child, 6th-7th century **19.** Gold Half Moon-Shaped Earring with Peacocks, late 6th-7th century **20.** Necklace with Gold Marriage Medallion and Hematite Amulet, 400–450 (medallion); 100–200 (amulet) **21.** Girdle with Coins and Medallions, ca. 583, reassembled after discovery **22.** Gold Necklace with Pendants, ca. 7th century **23.** Pectoral with Coins and Pseudo-Medallion, ca. 539–550 **24.** Clasp with

Intaglio Medallion of the Virgin and Child, 6th century **25.** Gold Cross Pendant, 500–700 **26.** Spherical Pendant or Button, 900–950 **27.** Cross with Pearls, 1200–1400 **28.** Gold "Basket" Earring, 6th century **29.** Gold Signet Ring of Michael Zorianos, ca. 1300 **30.** Finger Ring, 7th century **31.** Cross, ca. 1100 **32.** Circular Fragment with a Vine Scroll Motif, 1000–1100 **33.** Reliquary Finial, 9th–10th century **34.** Medallion of Saint Nicholas, 11th century **35.** Tip of a Pointer, 1080–1150 **36.** Plaque of Saint John, 12th century **37.** Silver Bucket, 600s **38.** The Attarouthi Treasure, Chalice, 500–650 **39.** Plate with Monogram, 610–613 **40.** The Attarouthi Treasure, Wine Strainer, 500–650 **41.** Plate with David Anointed by Samuel, 629–630 **42.** Silver Cross, 500–700 **43.** Silver Spoon, mid-6th–mid-7th century **44.** Flask with the Adoration of the Magi, 6th century **45.** Liturgical Knife, 6th century **46.** Pyxis with the Miracle of Christ's Multiplication of the Loaves, 6th century **47.** Pyx with the Women at Christ's Tomb, 6th century **48.** Panel from an Ivory Casket with the Story of Adam and Eve, 10th or 11th century **49.** Reliquary Casket with the Deesis, Archangels, 950–1000 **50.** Casket Plaque, 900–1000 **51.** Panel from an Ivory Casket with the Story of Adam and Eve, 10th or 11th century **52.** Casket with Warriors and Mythological Figures, 10th–11th century **53.** Fragment with Personification of the Nile, 6th century

Percussion

Drums were among the earliest instruments. They were used across cultures to accompany singing and dancing as well as on the battlefield. Many of the percussion instruments featured on this page were used in special ceremonies and rituals, like the sacred slit gong made by the latmul people of Papua New Guinea or the bronze bell of Zhou dynasty China, both pictured on the opposite page. Some were fashioned into fantastical shapes and adorned with elaborate figures, like the ones that surround the spider drum from Cameroon.

Percussion can be tuned, which means the instrument might have a range of pitches (such as the Bala from the Mandinka people) or a pitch that can be adjusted by the player, or it can be non-tuned (like the Sistrum rattle). The maker's materials and the size of the instrument affect its sound and tone; larger, deeper sounds are created by bigger drums and gongs. The wide range of natural materials featured in these instruments include lizard skin on the Asmat drum, sharkskin on the Pahu, and gourds, which are resonators on the Bala.

Slit Gong
(*Atingting Kon*)

Ambrym, Vanuatu,
mid- to late 1960s

Did you know?

The Gamelan is an orchestra of metal gongs and bells from Java and Indonesia, all tuned to different pitches. This Slento, an instrument used in Gamelan, has a frame shaped like a dragon.

Slento
Java, late 19th century

Drum

*Chief Omas,
Asmat people,
mid-20th century*

Drum (*Pahu*)

*Austral Islanders,
early 19th century*

Spider Drum

*Possibly Babungo/
Vengo people,
Cameroon,
ca. 1940*

**Miniature Drum
with Four Frogs**

*Vietnam, ca. 500
BCE–300 CE*

**Sacred Slit Gong
(*Waken*)**

*Latmul people,
19th century*

Drum

*Akan Ashanti people,
Ghana, early 20th
century*

Side Drum

Germany, 1694–1733

Bala

*Mandinka people,
Guinea, 19th century*

Densho

Japan, 19th century

Bell (*Zhong*)

*China, early 5th
century BCE*

Sistrum (Rattle)

Hattian, ca. 2300–2000 BCE

Wind Instruments

The selection of instruments on these pages includes pieces made from bone, wood, clay, and metal. The first flutes were made from animal bones. They were hollowed and modified to include finger holes to alter the pitch (which was made higher or lower by adding or taking away fingers).

Xun

China, 206 BCE–220 CE

This 2,000-year-old clay flute is an example of one of China's oldest instruments. Egg-shaped, it has a blowhole and finger holes to alter the pitch.

Limestone Aulos Player

Cyprus, 1st half of 6th century BCE

This limestone piper plays an aulos, an instrument popular in the ancient world, where two pipes, each with three or four finger holes, are blown at the same time. Like the modern oboe, the instrument's mouthpiece has a double reed—two thin pieces of wood, through which air vibrates.

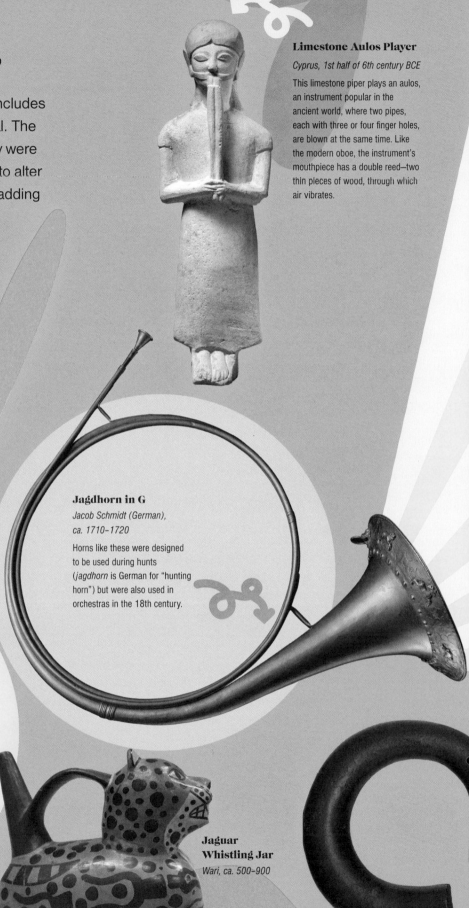

Jagdhorn in G

*Jacob Schmidt (German),
ca. 1710–1720*

Horns like these were designed to be used during hunts (*jagdhorn* is German for "hunting horn") but were also used in orchestras in the 18th century.

Did you know?

Ceramic "whistling jars" sculpted in the shape of animals and birds have been found across the Americas, and examples date back to as far as around 500 BCE. They feature one or two chambers that are partly filled with liquid. Sound is made when the jar is tipped in various directions, so that the water displaces the air out of the spout. This jaguar-shaped example from Peru features a spout on the back and another opening behind the creature's head.

Jaguar Whistling Jar

Wari, ca. 500–900

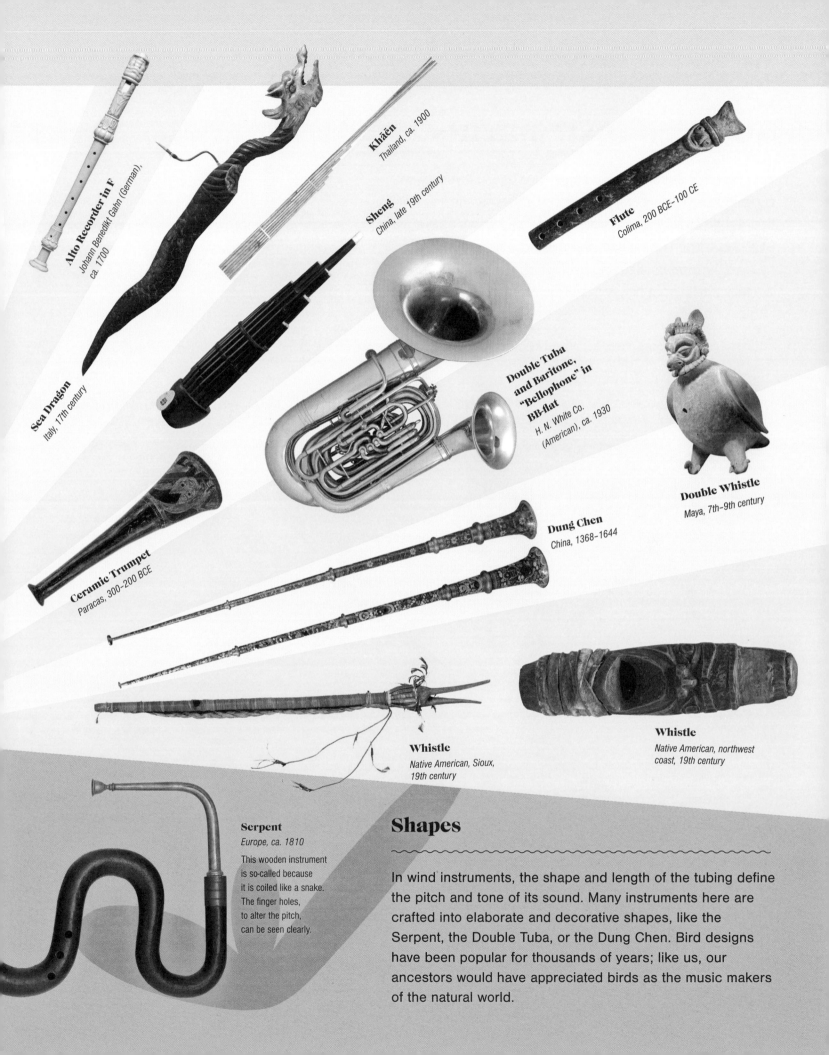

Alto Recorder in F
Johann Benedikt Gahn (German),
ca. 1700

Sea Dragon
Italy, 17th century

Khāēn
Thailand, ca. 1900

Sheng
China, late 19th century

Flute
Colima, 200 BCE–100 CE

**Double Tuba
and Baritone,
"Bellophone" in
BB-flat**
H. N. White Co.
(American), ca. 1930

Double Whistle
Maya, 7th–9th century

Ceramic Trumpet
Paracas, 300–200 BCE

Dung Chen
China, 1368–1644

Whistle
Native American, Sioux,
19th century

Whistle
Native American, northwest
coast, 19th century

Serpent
Europe, ca. 1810

This wooden instrument
is so-called because
it is coiled like a snake.
The finger holes,
to alter the pitch,
can be seen clearly.

Shapes

In wind instruments, the shape and length of the tubing define
the pitch and tone of its sound. Many instruments here are
crafted into elaborate and decorative shapes, like the
Serpent, the Double Tuba, or the Dung Chen. Bird designs
have been popular for thousands of years; like us, our
ancestors would have appreciated birds as the music makers
of the natural world.

Stringed Instruments

We know that stringed instruments have been played since ancient times. Single- and multi-stringed harps and lutes, like this arched shoulder harp from Egypt made about 1390–1295 BCE, have been found across the world, buried in tombs. Musical performers also appear in paintings and sculptures, like this female harp player from Tang dynasty China (right).

Arched Harp (Shoulder Harp)

Egypt, ca. 1390–1295 BCE

Carved wooden harps were popular instruments in ancient Egypt and appear in tomb paintings.

Female Musician with Harp

China, late 7th century

This clay musician plays a *konghou* (harp). She is from a set of female musicians playing different instruments. Musical groups frequently performed in the royal court during the Tang dynasty (618–907).

"The Antonius" Violin
Antonio Stradivari (Italian), ca. 1711

Mamadou Kouyaté with Bridge by Djimo Kouyaté, Kora
Mandinka people, ca. 1960

Murari Adhikari, Sitar
India, 1997

Pipa
China, late 16th–early 17th century

Lute
Pietro Railich (German), 1669

Sgra-Snyan
Tibet, 14th–16th century

Taūs (Mayuri)
India, 19th century

Gibson, Les Paul Prototype Recording Model, Serial no. 001
United States, 1982

The lute is a stringed instrument that is played with the fingers.

Double Virginal

Lodewijck Grouwels (Flemish), 1600

Spinet

Italy, 1540

Did you know?

Italian inventor Bartolomeo Cristofori designed the first successful hammer-action keyboard instrument, the piano, around 1700. The piano is a stringed instrument; when its keys are pressed, hammers inside strike the strings to produce a sound. Unlike the earlier harpsichord, virginal, and spinet, in which the strings are plucked, his new instrument allowed the player to strike the note softly (in Italian, *piano*) or loudly (*forte*)—hence the name, *pianoforte* (soft-loud).

Historically, strings were often made from silk in Asia, and in Africa, from twisted hide. In Europe, strings were often made from gut—tightly wound animal intestines! Today, they continue to be made from a variety of materials, including metal and nylon. The length and tension of strings affect the sound—a tighter, shorter string produces a higher-pitched note. Strings are often attached to a sound box made of wood, gourd, or metal that resonates (increases the volume of the sound) when the strings are plucked or bowed. On many electric stringed instruments, such as the Les Paul guitar, the body is solid, and the sound is produced when it is plugged into an amplifier.

Grand Piano

Bartolomeo Cristofori (Italian), 1720

This is the oldest of the three surviving pianos by Cristofori.

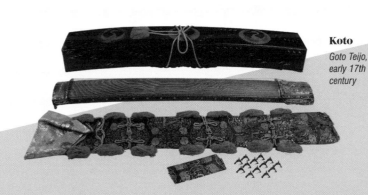

Koto

Goto Teijo, early 17th century

Kerar (Lyre)

Ethiopia or Sudan, early to mid-20th century

Trade

During the Middle Ages, Asia was teeming with traders transporting their wares. They would travel far and wide, across land and sea, to exchange goods with people from other regions. A sprawling network of trade routes joined East and Southern Asia with the Middle East, Africa, and Europe. There were deserts, storms, bandits, and other threats to face, but it was worth it for those who made a profit!

Did you know?

As well as transporting valuable items, Silk Road travelers carried ideas. These included techniques for cultivating, ways to make textiles and paper, and discoveries in science and astronomy. Traders also shared languages and religions as they chatted with people from foreign lands. Buddhism, for example, spread quickly from India to Central Asia, China, and beyond.

The Silk Road

One of the most important trade networks in history was the Silk Road, which was about 4,000 miles (6,437 km) long. Precious silk from China was carried along it as long ago as the 100s BCE. Gems, food, spices, luxury items, and other things soon joined the loads traveling back and forth. Cities grew up along the routes, with bustling markets where merchants bartered. Silk Road business boomed until 1453, when the Ottomans (see page 105) closed off trade with the West. After that, European traders mainly took to the sea.

Rafter Finial in the Shape of a Dragon's Head and Wind Chime
Korea, 10th century

Buddhism reached Korea via China in the 4th century and was thriving by the time this dragon was made. Korean dragons were symbols of protection. This one probably guarded a Buddhist temple.

Dish with Recumbent Elephant Surrounded by Clouds
Vietnam, 15th–16th century

Thanks to the Silk Road, designs from one region often mixed with techniques from another. From its style, we know this bowl is Vietnamese, but it uses cobalt blue on white porcelain, a technique that originated in China.

Table Screen with Landscape

China, second half 15th century

The cloisonné enameling technique of this Chinese table screen originated in the Byzantine Empire but was transformed by Chinese artisans.

Back **Front**

Safe Conduct Pass (*Paiza*) with Inscription in Phakpa Script

China, late 13th century

This Safe Conduct Pass granted its owner the right to travel, trade, and lodge in Mongol lands. The Mongols ruled a vast empire, covering most Silk Road territory, from 1206 until 1328.

Silk and Paper

The earliest surviving fragments of silk are nearly 5,000 years old! They were made of fine threads from the cocoon of the silkworm. Several of these threads were twisted together by hand and then woven on a loom. People wrote documents and painted pictures on long scrolls of silk. This continued even after a cheaper invention, paper, began to change the world. Paper was first made in China around 105 CE. In later centuries, paper was used for printed books, banknotes, and even tea bags and toilet paper, but artists still loved painting on silk.

Elegant Gathering in the Apricot Garden

China, ca. 1437

The colors used in silk paintings like this came from natural pigments, including cinnabar (red) and azurite (blue). Yellow pigments, such as orpiment and gamboge, were bright but also toxic.

Finches and Bamboo

China, early 12th century

The textured surface of silk made it an ideal ground for applying mineral pigments. The fineness of its weave also enabled artists to add intricate details, like the feathers on these beautiful finches.

Brush and Ink

Painting was done with a brush and ink—the same tools used for writing. Animal hair formed the tip of the brush, while the handle was made of wood or bamboo. Black ink came from soot mixed with glue, which hardened into a solid stick. Artists ground this into powder on an ink stone and mixed it with water to dilute it to the right shade.

Writing Brush with Geometric Patterns

China, 13th century

Making Paper

Early paper was made from the bark of the mulberry tree. It was soaked and pounded into a pulp, then dried in sheets on wooden frames or screens. Adding hemp and old rags to the pulp created a higher-quality paper. Over the centuries, paper makers tried many different fibers, including grass, bamboo, rice, and even seaweed.

Musk Cat

Japan, mid–late 16th century

This Japanese paper scroll shows an impressive range of brushstrokes, from the thick, flowing lines of the branches to the super-fine bristles of the cat's fur!

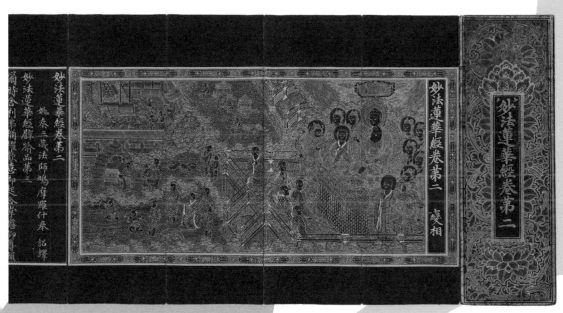

Illustrated Manuscript of the Lotus Sutra (*Miaofa Lianhua Jing*), Volume 2

Korea, ca. 1340

Gold pigments really gleam on the indigo-dyed mulberry paper of this Korean Buddhist manuscript.

Grooms and Horses

China, 1296 and 1359

Handscrolls like this one were usually kept in a box and unrolled from right to left for viewing. This revealed sections of the painting one by one, a bit like turning the pages of a book. The red stamps, called seals, are the marks of the artist or of different collectors who owned the scroll.

Protective Deities and Guardians

Guardian figures watched silently and faithfully over temples, tombs, and homes in Asia. Often, they took the form of stone statues flanking doorways, warding off evil with a weapon or a glare. People of different faiths believed in a wide range of protective gods and goddesses. These heroic deities usually had human or animal characteristics as well as their own divine powers.

One of the Four Heavenly Kings
Japan, 12th century

Guardian lions

Lions are known as the king of the beasts—they represent strength and courage and have long been seen as symbols of power. Lions were often shown supporting the throne of Buddha. Pairs of guardian lions stood proudly at the entrances of royal palaces, temples, and shrines.

Guardian Lion

Cambodia or Thailand, 11th–early 12th century

Anyone approaching a Khmer temple in Cambodia would have met a mighty lion like this one. As well as being a symbol of power, the lion was a personal symbol of the Khmer kings, who were believed to be gods themselves.

Watchful Kings

The Four Heavenly Kings guarded the four quarters of the world—north, south, east, and west. They were originally Hindu gods, but soon became protectors of Buddhists and Buddhism too. In Korea and China, they greeted visitors to temples as huge statues or paintings on the gates. In Japan, they often surrounded the main altar, like the carved figure seen here. Each king carried his own emblematic object, usually a pagoda, a sword, a lute, and a snakelike dragon.

The Buddhist Guardian Mahabala

Indonesia (Java), 11th century

Mahabala, the conqueror of death, shows his power by trampling the enemy. This Indonesian bronze statue of a Buddhist deity has six heads and six arms and legs.

Zaō Gongen

Japan, 14th century

This lively spirit, Zaō Gongen, was protector of a sacred mountain in Japan. He was worshiped by people of the Shinto religion. This figure would have once held a thunderbolt in his right hand; fragile pieces like this can break off over the years and are often missing from very old sculptures. Experts identify parts that have been lost by studying history and other artworks.

Water-Moon Avalokiteshvara

Korea, first half 14th century

Korean Buddhists believed that the Water-Moon Avalokiteshvara prevented calamity and disease. He also safeguarded travelers on their journeys, like the small figures at the bottom of this painting.

Buddhism in the Himalayas

The highest Buddhist monasteries in the world are found in the Himalayan mountains! Buddhism arrived here via gurus, or Buddhist masters, who visited from India. Travelers from Tibet also discovered the faith in India and brought it back home. By the middle of the 11th century, Buddhism was the most popular religion in Tibet. People in this area made the faith their own by merging it with native beliefs. The Buddhism that they practiced, known as Vajrayana, is still widespread in the Himalayas today.

Did you know?

Vajrayana Buddhists use many rituals, which are explained in texts called *tantras*. They include meditation, yoga, and *mantras*—sounds or words that are repeated in a chant. These techniques help believers focus their mind, contact spirits, and work toward enlightenment. Vajrayana Buddhists believe that anyone can achieve enlightenment in their lifetime if they really try.

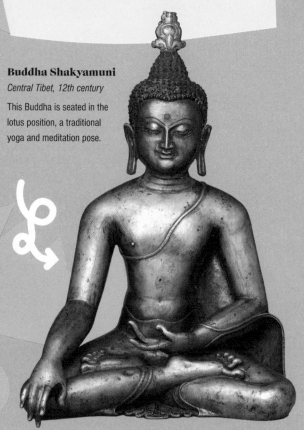

Buddha Shakyamuni
Central Tibet, 12th century
This Buddha is seated in the lotus position, a traditional yoga and meditation pose.

Mandala of Jnanadakini
Tibet, late 14th century
This colorful mandala is centered on the six-armed goddess Jnanadakini.

The Mandala

Every Tibetan Buddhist monk is trained in making a mandala. This is a kind of symbolic map of the universe and the realm of the gods. It can be painted on paper or cloth, drawn in colored sand, or even made of wood or stone. Usually, it is based on a series of circles and squares contained inside one another. Mandalas are used in meditation, drawing a person's gaze to a central deity. The idea is to free the mind of everyday clutter and fill it with spiritual calm.

The Bodhisattva Manjushri as a Youth
Nepal, 10th century

Vajrayana Buddhists believe in bodhisattvas, enlightened beings who stayed on Earth to guide others. Manjushri, who represented wisdom, was a popular bodhisattva in Nepal.

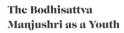

Portrait of Jnanatapa Attended by Lamas and Mahasiddhas
Eastern Tibet, ca. 1350

This painting, created for a monastery in Tibet, shows various monks and deities surrounding a great leader.

Initiation Cards (Tsakalis)
Tibet, 15th century

Traveling teachers used cards like these to summon and introduce different deities. The portable cards could be laid down in the shape of a mandala.

Porcelain

Potters experimented with many types of clay before they discovered porcelain. This mixed material, invented in China nearly 2,000 years ago, was the hardest, finest ceramic known. It could be molded into delicate shapes and was translucent white when fired. This made it perfect for decorating with paints and glazes, from cobalt blue to celadon green.

1. Dish with Design of Hare in Clouds, Japan, ca. 1624–1643 **2.** Dish with Cherry Blossoms, Japan, mid-17th century **3.** Dog, Japan, late 17th century **4.** Deep Dish with Egret (from a set of ten), Japan, 1639 **5.** Jar with Lid, Korea, 15th–16th century **6.** Wine Cup with Ear Handles, Korea, 15th century **7.** Dish, Korea, second half 15th century **8.** Small Bowl Decorated with Chrysanthemum, Korea, 12th century **9.** Altar Bowl with Winged Animals among Waves, China, mid-15th century **10.** Flask with Medallion, China, early 15th century **11.** Chrysanthemum-Petal Dish with Tortoise, Cranes, and Flowers, China, 12th–early 13th century **12.** Jar with Winged Animals over Waves, China, mid-15th century **13.** Dish, China, early 15th century **14.** Vase with horses in waves, China, mid-14th century

11   12   13   14   15   16   17

18   19   20   21   22

23   24   25   26   27   28   29   30

31   32   33   34   35   36   37   38   39

40   41   42   43   44   45   46

15. Ewer with Cover, China, 12th century **16.** Ewer with Lotus Petal Collar, Vietnam, 11th–12th century **17.** Bowl with Plum Blossom and Crescent Moon, China, late 13th–14th century **18.** Pair of vases: Qingbai Shufu-type ware, China, 14th century **19.** Incense Burner in Shape of Lion (one of a pair), China, early 14th century **20.** Stem Cup, China, ca. first half 14th century **21.** Pillow in Shape of Reclining Woman, China, 12th–13th century **22.** Altar bowl with Tibetan inscription, China, early 15th century **23.** Bottle with vegetal scrolls, China, late 13th century **24.** Seated bodhisattva, China, late 13th–early 14th century **25.** Jar with immortals, China, late 15th century **26.** Vase, China, first half 14th century **27.** Meiping Vase, China, early 15th century **28.** Plate with Lotus, China, 15th century **29.** Foliated plate with rocks, plants, and melons, China, 14th century **30.** Jar, China, 11th–12th century **31.** Vase in Meiping Shape with Daoist Immortal Zhongli Quan, China, second half 15th century **32.** Jar with peony scroll, China, 14th century **33.** Plate with Carp, China, mid-14th century **34.** Monk's cap ewer, China, early 15th century **35.** Basin with Lotus Pond, China, late 15th century **36.** Vase in Shape of Ancient Bronze Vessel, China, 15th–16th century **37.** Faceted Vase, China, ca. first half 14th century **38.** Dish with Blossoming Plum and Crescent Moon, China, mid–late 15th century **39.** Vase, China, 11th–12th century **40.** Flask with Lotus Pond, China, mid-14th century **41.** Bowl with Peonies, Narcissus, and Pomegranates, China, early 15th century **42.** Bowl with Chrysanthemums, China, late 14th century **43.** Bottle with Peony Scroll, China, mid-14th century **44.** Dish with Scalloped Rim, China, 11th century **45.** Stem Bowl, China, mid-14th century **46.** Bowl, China, 12th–13th century

Medieval Europe

The art of medieval Europe was eye-catching and colorful. It was full of expression and narrative detail, often celebrating the prestige of the artwork's owner. Most art was made in skilled craft workshops for rich buyers, called patrons. Nobles with grand castles, and the wealthy Catholic Church, drove the art styles and subjects of the time.

Around 1000 CE, builders developed a new style of architecture that used round stone arches—a style people today call Romanesque because it was partly inspired by ancient Rome. In the mid-1100s, the Gothic style emerged, with pointed arches and elaborate detail.

The Coronation of the Virgin, and Saints

Giovanni di Tano Fei (Italian), 1394

This Gothic altarpiece shows Christ crowning his mother, Mary, surrounded by saints and prophets. In medieval art, important figures like these were usually bigger than others, such as the angels in the foreground.

The Intercession of Christ and the Virgin

Lorenzo Monaco (Piero di Giovanni) (Italian), before 1402

Notice the tiny praying figures kneeling here at the feet of a much larger Christ.

Annunciation Triptych (Merode Altarpiece)

Workshop of Robert Campin (Netherlandish), ca. 1427–1432

This ground-breaking painting placed holy figures in an ordinary 15th-century townhouse. Look at all the detail, from pots to mousetraps, in the home of Mary and her carpenter husband, Joseph.

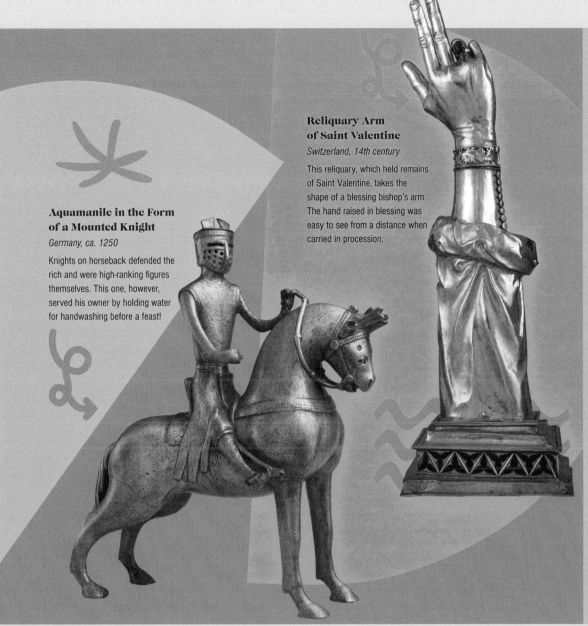

Patrons and Pilgrims

The Church was by far the biggest patron of art in medieval Europe. It made money from taxes and donations from the people and became extremely powerful. New churches and cathedrals needed furnishing and decorating. Monasteries also generated art. Many monks and nuns were skilled artists, creating books as well as other works of art.

Pilgrims are people who visit saints' tombs and remains. The treasured remains, or relics, of the saints were displayed in special containers called *reliquaries*, which were often made from precious metals and adorned with gems.

Reliquary Arm of Saint Valentine
Switzerland, 14th century

This reliquary, which held remains of Saint Valentine, takes the shape of a blessing bishop's arm. The hand raised in blessing was easy to see from a distance when carried in procession.

Aquamanile in the Form of a Mounted Knight
Germany, ca. 1250

Knights on horseback defended the rich and were high-ranking figures themselves. This one, however, served his owner by holding water for handwashing before a feast!

Layers of Life

The majority of people in medieval Europe were farmers who worked the land. They had little compared to the noble landowners who lived in castles or manor houses. City dwellers often became craftspeople or worked as butchers, bakers, roofers, and more. As time went by, some made enough money to buy art like the wealthier classes.

Life in a rich household typically included pastimes such as hunting, feasting, and listening to music. This led to the creation of splendid tableware, instruments, and other decorative objects. Sporting scenes, battles, and fabulous animals appeared in pictures and carvings. Pleasure gardens, like colorful private parks, were also popular.

Arch with Beasts
France, ca. 1150–1175
The smooth curve of this Romanesque arch is carved with fantastic beasts. Medieval people loved *bestiaries*—illustrated books that described both real and mythical animals and their traits.

Stained-Glass Windows

The power and wealth of the Church in the Middle Ages were clear for all to see. Great cathedrals, taking decades to build, towered over everything in the landscape. The interiors of these mighty buildings were bathed in light from magnificent stained-glass windows. Colorful scenes and characters from the Bible glistened as the sun shone through.

Stained glass also began to appear in wealthy homes and public buildings—often to celebrate family histories or events, or simply as lavish decoration.

A Teaching Tool

Stained-glass windows weren't just popular for their beauty—they also had a practical purpose. Most ordinary people in medieval Europe were unable to read or write. Church windows flourished because they helped illustrate Bible stories. Worshipers could picture the saints and prophets as they listened to sermons and readings from the gospels.

The light from stained-glass windows was seen as a sign that God was near. It tied in with the Christian message of leading people out of darkness into light.

Cathedrals in the Middle Ages were often built with stained-glass windows.

Theodosius Arrives at Ephesus, from a Scene from the Legend of the Seven Sleepers of Ephesus
France, ca. 1200–1210

Copper-based red glass always came out very dark, so it let very little light through. Glassmakers later solved this by dipping clear glass into copper, producing more luminous "flashed glass."

Roundel with Playing at Quintain
France, ca. 1500

From the 1400s, plain panes of glass were often painted and silver-stained for private houses. These two figures are trying to topple each other in a medieval balancing game!

The Mater Dolorosa
Lautenbach Master (German), ca. 1480

Glass was made from a mix of sand and potash (a type of salt that, at this time, was made from wood or plant ash). The mix was melted into liquid and then cooled. To color it, powdered metals were added, such as cobalt for blue or copper for red. The term *stained glass* comes from silver staining, invented in the 1300s. This involved painting silver nitrate on glass to create golden tones, as seen in this halo.

Quatrefoil Roundel with Arms and Secular Scenes
Germany, 1490–1500

This secular window may have lit up a royal residence because it shows the Austrian Empire's coat of arms. Around it are scenes of a jousting tournament—a popular pastime in medieval courts.

Scenes from the Legend of Saint Vincent of Saragossa and the History of His Relics
France, ca. 1245–1247

This jewel-like window tells the story of Saint Vincent, whom we see taken prisoner near the top. The two kings on horseback are transporting his relics to a French abbey built in his honor.

Window Making

Assembling a stained-glass window began with a design drawn onto a large board. The glazier would lay a sheet of colored glass on top and use a hot iron, followed by cool water, to cut out the shapes. Details and shading were painted on and then fired to set the paint. Next, grooved strips of lead called *cames* were wrapped around the glass and fixed in place. The pieces were carefully joined like a jigsaw and waterproofed with putty under the cames. Finally, the panel was secured in an iron frame before being mounted in the window.

Adoration of the Magi
Germany, 1507

Medieval glass paint was usually brown or dark gray. It allowed artists to add intricate detail. The textures of hair, straw, and fabrics in this scene showing the Magi adoring Jesus were all painted on with a fine brush.

Illuminated Manuscripts

Before the printing press was invented in the 1440s, books were written and decorated by hand. These handmade books were incredible works of art. Known as *manuscripts*, meaning "written by hand," they were usually decorated—or illuminated—with gold. Illuminated manuscripts took teams of craftspeople many months or even years to complete. Often, they were made by monks who worked only in daylight to avoid candle fires.

Most illuminated manuscripts were religious texts, read in churches and monasteries. Rulers and nobles commissioned them, too, especially prayer books known as Books of Hours.

The Belles Heures of Jean de France, duc de Berry

The Limbourg Brothers (Franco-Netherlandish), 1405–1408/09

The Limbourg brothers excelled at painting miniatures. There are 172 in this Book of Hours! The three brothers illuminated this manuscript when they were in their teens and early 20s. The wealthy duke who owned it soon ordered another book, but he and the Limbourg brothers died before it was finished, probably of the plague.

Monk-Scribe Astride a Wyvern
Germany, mid-12th century

Parchment Pages

The pages of a manuscript were made of animal hides that had been soaked, scraped, and then stretched out to dry. This created parchment (or vellum, if it was calfskin), which produced a higher-quality surface. The parchment was folded in half to form a *bifolio*—two leaves making up four pages. These were later stacked into groups, called gatherings, and sewn onto leather supports. Pages were marked with evenly ruled lines, then smoothed with pumice or chalk. Black ink for writing was usually made from ground gallnuts—natural growths found on the bark of trees.

Team Effort

The writer, or scribe, wrote with a quill pen made from a goose or swan feather. They corrected mistakes by scraping off letters or crossing out words and rewriting them in the margin. They might make notes for the rubricator, who wrote headings in red ink. Then, it was time for the illuminator to sketch out the decoration. A gilder painted on sticky binder and laid gold leaf on top. The painting was done using vivid pigments from plants, minerals, stones, insects, and even horse dung. This was often polished for shine using an animal tooth. Finally, the bookbinder fastened the gatherings into a leather cover.

Manuscript Leaf with Scenes from the Life of Saint Francis of Assisi

Italy, ca. 1320–1342

Burnished gold leaf lights up these pictures from the story of Saint Francis of Assisi. In every scene, a gleaming halo surrounds Saint Francis's head.

Manuscript Illumination with the Annunciation in an Initial R, from a Gradual

Switzerland, ca. 1300

The first letter of a page was often large and extravagant, like this R from the opening of a hymn. Under its arch, we see the Angel Gabriel telling the Virgin Mary that she will be the mother of Jesus.

Manuscript Leaf with Initial A, from a Gradual

Germany, first half 15th century

This is the music of a psalm, often played on the first Sunday of Advent. The biblical king David is shown within the letter A, playing a stringed instrument called a psaltery.

Book-Cover Plaque with Christ in Majesty

France, ca. 1200

This enameled plaque was attached to a book cover, creating a luxurious finish. The winged man, lion, ox, and eagle are symbols of the four evangelists: Matthew, Mark, Luke, and John.

Leaf from a Beatus Manuscript: the Lamb at the Foot of the Cross, Flanked by Two Angels

Spain, ca. 1180

Illuminators outlined their work in bold colors to make it stand out on the page. The lines here provide texture to the angels' wings and clothing, as well as the Lamb of God's fleece.

Medieval Tapestries

The ancient art of tapestry weaving became big business in medieval churches and castles. Tapestries could decorate and divide a vast room as well as help keep it warm! These precious works of art and insulation were hugely time-consuming to produce. A tapestry of 10 sq ft (1 sq m) took at least a month to weave, and some tapestries were 30 ft (9 m) long. Tapestries were easy to roll and transport between a rich owner's different houses. Sometimes, they were won in battle and then were altered to fit their new homes.

The Weaving Process

Tapestry weaving started with a *cartoon*—a full-size colored drawing or painting. This was placed behind a wooden weaving loom, which had strong threads called warps stretched across it. The weaver wove colored threads called wefts through the warps, following the design on the cartoon. When finished, the tapestry was flipped over, so the front was a mirror image of the cartoon.

Several weavers could work together, side by side, at a large loom. Most tapestry yarn was made of wool or silk, dyed with plant or insect colors. Sometimes more valuable silver or other metallic threads were woven in.

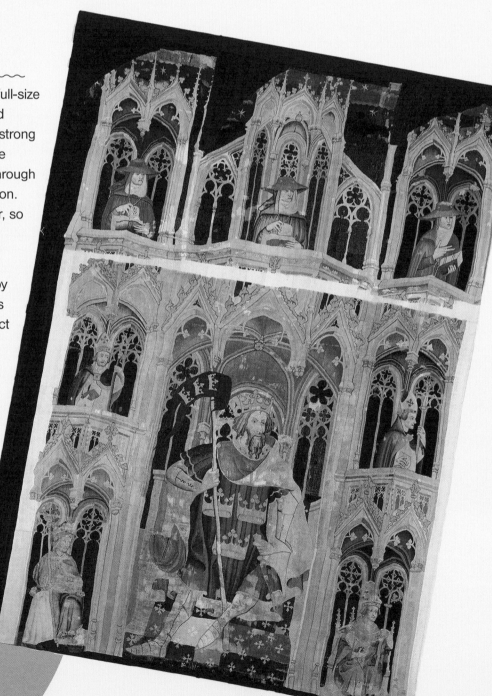

King Arthur (from the Nine Heroes Tapestries)
South Netherlandish, ca. 1400
The detail in tapestries was often spread out in a pattern, like this one from the South Netherlands.

The Unicorn Purifies Water, from the Unicorn Tapestries
France (cartoon); Southern Netherlands (woven) ca. 1495–1505

The mythical unicorn was famed in the Middle Ages as a symbol of purity. Here, it cleanses a stream with its horn, surrounded by sage, orange, and other plants that were used as antidotes to poison.

A Booming Industry

The tapestry industry boomed from the 1300s, especially in northern France and the southern Netherlands. Here, skilled weavers and dyers from the cloth trade helped boost both quality and quantity. Local groups called *guilds* supported the craft, providing training and monitoring prices. There were guilds of all kinds, from candlemakers to bookbinders, with apprentices working toward becoming masters.

Patrons who were rich enough to commission tapestries often chose mythical or biblical subjects. Battles, hunting scenes, and heroic figures were also popular.

Garden: A Lady and Two Gentlemen
South Netherlandish, ca. 1440–1450

These colors and emblems suggest that the tapestry belonged to the French King Charles VII. The clothing, jewelry, and even the roses have expensive metallic threads woven in.

Bear Hunt
Flemish, ca. 1470–1490

Tapestry cartoons were often reused to create multiple versions of a design. This drawing seems to be a copy of a cartoon, with some of the details changed to update it.

The Battle with the Sagittary and the Conference at Achilles' Tent, from Scenes from the Story of the Trojan War
South Netherlandish, ca. 1470–1490

The chaos of battle is brilliantly captured in these tightly crammed, overlapping figures. They're fighting the Trojan War, more than 2,500 years before the tapestry was made, yet the armor is medieval.

Tapestry with the Annunciation
South Netherlandish, ca. 1410–1420

Blues, like the Virgin Mary's dress here, were usually made from the leaves of the woad plant, which can be used to produce a blue dye. The root of the madder plant produced a range of pinks and reds, as did cochineal—a dye made from dried beetles.

Pouring and Storing

Medieval banquets needed pitchers for wine and aquamaniles for handwashing water. Kitchens and pharmacies used so many storage jars that their decoration helped distinguish their purpose on the shelf.

1

2

3

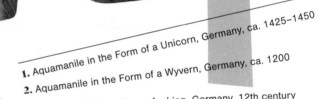

1. Aquamanile in the Form of a Unicorn, Germany, ca. 1425–1450

2. Aquamanile in the Form of a Wyvern, Germany, ca. 1200

3. Aquamanile in the Form of a Lion, Germany, 12th century

4. Aquamanile in the Form of a Rooster, Germany, 13th century

5. Aquamanile in the Form of a Lion, Germany, ca. 1400

6. Aquamanile in the Form of a Horse, Germany, ca. 1400

4

5

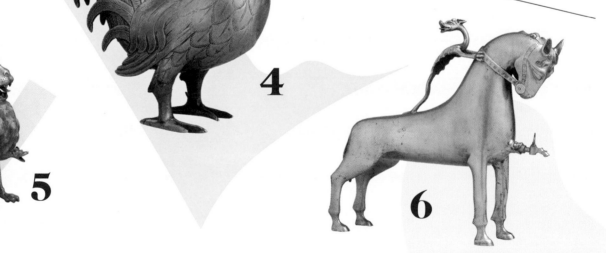

6

7. Ewer, late 15th century 8. Drinking Bowl, second half 15th century 9. Jasper Cup with Gilded-Silver Mounts, ca. 1350–1380 10. Turret Laver, 15th century 11. Ewer, late 15th–early 16th century 13. Pharmacy Jar, 1435–1465 14. Pharmacy Jar, first half 15th century 15. Jug, second half 15th century 16. Storage Jar (*albarello*) with a Profile Portrait, ca. 1480–1500 17. Pharmacy Jar, 15th century 18. Pharmacy Jar, 15th century 19. Storage Jar (*albarello*) Depicting a Peacock, ca. 1470–1500 20. Jug, ca. 1480–1500 21. Storage Jar (*albarello*), ca. 1480–1500 22. Two-Handled Storage Jug (*albarello*) with Crowned Eagles, ca. 1460–1480 23. Ewer, late 15th–early 16th century 24. Ewer or cruet, late 15th or early 16th century 25. Armorial Jug (*boccale*), late 15th century 26. Armorial Jug (*boccale*), ca. 1470–1480 28. Armorial Jug (*boccale*), ca. 1460–1480 29. Spouted Jug, ca. 1500 30. Pharmacy Jar, early 15th century 31. Jug with Finely Dressed Woman, 1430–1440 32. Albarello, ca. 1480 33. Two-Handled Jar with Birds and a Coat of Arms, early 1400s 34. Albarello, ca. 1475

7 **8** **9** **10** **11**

12
Double Cup
Prague, second half 15th century
The top half of a double cup served as a lid but could also be removed and used separately.

13 **14** **15**

16 **17** **18** **19** **20**

21 **22** **23**

24 **25** **26**

27 Two-Handled Pharmacy or Storage Jar with Arms of the Orsini Family and Profile of a Man
Italy, ca. 1460–1480

Numbers scratched into the bottom of a storage jar like this one noted its weight when empty (see below). This was useful when it came to measuring contents.

28 **29** **30**

39 Pharmacy Jar
Italy, ca. 1470–1490
Designing jars with a handle at the back helped them fit side by side on a shelf.

31

32 **33** **34** **35** **36** **37** **38** **40**

41 **42** **43** **44** **45** **46** **47** **48** **49** **50**

51 **52** **53** **54** **55** **56** **57** **58** **59** **60** **61** **62**

35. Armorial Jug (boccale), late 15th century **36.** Jug with Eagle, early 15th century **37.** Jug with Figure in Profile, 1420–1450 **38.** Jar, 13th century **40.** Jug, ca. 1400 **41.** Pharmacy Jar, 1400–1450 **42.** Jug, 15th century **43.** Jug, 15th century **44.** Jug with Applied Decoration, 13th century **45.** Jug with Horseshoes, 13th century **46.** Cup, 15th century **47.** Pharmacy Jar, 15th century **48.** Jug, late 15th or early 16th century **49.** Jug, 15th century **50.** Pitcher, ca. 1100–1150 **51.** Barrel-Shaped Jug with a Fox and a Rooster, late 13th century **52.** Jug with Flattened Spout, ca. 1300 **53.** Pitcher, ca. 1430 **54.** Pitcher, 13th century **55.** Cup, 15th century **56.** Cup, 15th century **57.** Jug, first half 14th century **58.** Jug, late 13th–early 14th century **59.** Jug, late 13th–early 14th century **60.** Jar, 13th–14th century **61.** Pharmacy Jar (albarello), ca. 1475–1500 **62.** Pharmacy Jar (albarello), ca. 1475–1500

Playing Cards

Believed to have originated in China during the Southern Song dynasty (1127–1279), playing cards became popular in India and Persia (modern-day Iran) and then in Egypt. During the second half of the 14th century, they arrived in Europe. Though card playing was widely enjoyed by all levels of society, some of the earliest surviving decks (like the ones pictured on these pages) were expensive, hand-painted works of art, affordable only for wealthy patrons, such as members of the ruling class.

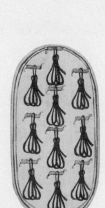

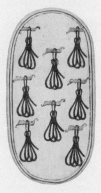
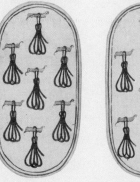

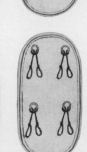

Queen of Nooses, from The Cloisters Playing Cards
South Netherlandish, ca. 1475–1480

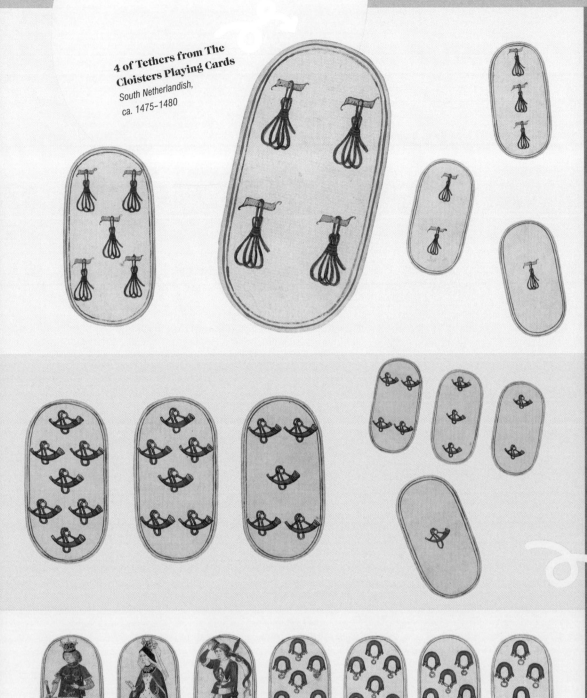

4 of Tethers from The Cloisters Playing Cards
South Netherlandish, ca. 1475–1480

The Cloisters Playing Cards

These pages show cards in the collection of The Met Cloisters. These oval cards were handmade in the Netherlands during the 15th century. The set contains four suits, each based on equipment used during a hunt (hunting horns, dog collars, hound tethers, and game nooses). Within each suit is a finely dressed king, queen, and knave, along with 10 number cards.

Knave of Horns, from The Cloisters Playing Cards
South Netherlandish, ca. 1475–1480

3. APPROACHING THE MODERN ERA

Landscapes of East Asia

Throughout history, artists and craftsmen across East Asia have produced images of the natural world, from paintings to wood carvings and calligraphy to ceramics. Ink was painted on paper or silk and made into scrolls or folding screens.

Did you know?

Gongbi is a detailed technique of Chinese painting, and *xieyi* is a free, sketchy style. Artists using the gongbi technique worked carefully, using bright colors and small brushstrokes. Artists working in the xieyi style worked quickly, with light, loose marks. *Shui-mo* was ink wash, like watercolor painting.

Old Trees, Level Distance
Guo Xi (Chinese), ca. 1080

Guo Xi was an important Chinese landscape painter in the late 11th century. His paintings of different seasons and times of day convey distinct moods. In this somber autumn scene, two old men are about to say farewell as one prepares to retire. The leafless foreground trees, connected at their roots, suggest the men's lasting bond of friendship.

Orchid Pavilion Gathering
Ike Taiga (Japanese), ca. 1763

This folding screen was painted by the artist Taiga, who was famous in Japan for his calligraphic painting style. This screen depicts a poetry competition.

Dragon Pine

China, ca. 1400

This twisting pine tree resembles a coiling dragon rising into the sky. Pines, which remain green through the winter, were emblems of survival and became symbols of an individual's moral fortitude.

Wild Geese Descending to Sandbar

Korea, late 15th–early 16th century

This river valley with distant mountains and a flock of flying geese was painted by a Korean artist. In Korea, delicate ink paintings of landscapes were extremely popular in the 15th and 16th centuries.

Lacquer

A shiny coating called *lacquer* was applied to hard materials, such as wood or metal. It was made from the resin or sap of the lacquer tree. Much Asian lacquerware made during the 11th to 16th centuries was intricate and colorful and included objects such as boxes, trays, and even helmets.

Trefoil-Shaped Covered Box with Decoration of Chrysanthemums

Korea, ca. 12th century

A *trefoil* describes a three-leaved plant. The design of three overlapping circles, called a trefoil-shape, was popular in art and architecture during the Middle Ages. This trefoil-shaped box is decorated with patterns of chrysanthemums and other flowers made out of mother-of-pearl.

Stationery Box Decorated with Peony Scrolls

Korea, 15th–16th century

During the 15th and 16th centuries, Korean gentlemen often kept their paper and writing equipment in fancy boxes like this. This was first inlaid with tiny pieces of iridescent mother-of-pearl, set in elaborate repeating patterns of a peony and its leaf.

Helmet (Zukinnari Kabuto)

Japan, 16th century

In Japan, this square helmet was usually worn by older men, doctors, and priests. The top of it is covered in gold lacquer made in a technique called *tataki-nuri*. On the front, the dramatic crest, also made with red and gold lacquer, represents a Buddhist god surrounded by flames.

The Use of Lacquer

Lacquer was first used in China thousands of years ago, first on food utensils and then on pots, jugs, and bowls that were used in ceremonies and rituals. The use of lacquer spread to Korea and then Japan, and it became used for decoration on carriages, ceremonial weapons, buildings, and musical instruments. The earliest lacquerware was black and red, and then later, gold was used. By the 13th century, inlaid shell was part of many lacquered designs.

Sake Ewer (*Hisage*) with Chrysanthemums and Paulownia Crests in Alternating Fields

Japan, early 17th century

More than 400 years old, this round wooden jug was lacquered in "the Kōdaiji style," which features big bold patterns. Even though this was an everyday household object, the diagonal lines and simplified flower designs in gold, bronze, and black are elegant and sophisticated.

Tray with Women and Boys on a Garden Terrace

China, 14th century

This large red lacquered tray is in relief, meaning that the carved image is raised higher than the background (like a flat sculpture). The scene is of busy, happy family life in China, with mothers watching their children play games.

The Great Wave

Oceans and waves have been important in Japanese art for centuries and were depicted by many of Japan's most famous artists. Scenes of the sea were painted and printed on screens, fans, scrolls, and more. In the 1830s, Katsushika Hokusai made woodblock prints depicting a huge wave. It became one of the most famous works of art in the world.

Under the Wave off Kanagawa

Katsushika Hokusai (Japanese),
ca. 1830–1832

Hokusai created this woodblock print of a great wave overshadowing fishermen and Mount Fuji, Japan's most sacred mountain. It is part of his series of prints he called Thirty-Six Views of Mount Fuji, and it shows the great wave moments before it crashes down onto three tiny fishing boats below. In the background, Mount Fuji looks smaller than the waves.

Rough Waters

Ogata Korin (Japanese),
ca. 1704–1709

Ogata Korin painted these crashing waves on a folding screen, making the foam crests look like the long claws of a watery dragon. In some parts of the painting, Korin used the ancient Chinese technique of drawing with two brushes held together in one hand.

Girls Gathering Shells on the Sea-shore

Kitagawa Utamaro (Japanese), ca. 1790

Kitagawa Utamaro was one of the few ukiyo-e artists to become famous in his lifetime. This scene shows young ladies looking for shells by the sea. Notice the girls in the far distance, the tiny boats on the sea, and the young ladies chatting nearby.

Monk Nichiren Calming the Stormy Sea

Utagawa Kuniyoshi (Japanese), ca. 1835

Nichiren was the founder of a Buddhist sect. This print shows a dramatic event from his life, when he was in a fishing boat that became caught in a storm. While the fishermen believed they would all drown, Nichiren prayed, and the sea became calm.

Woodblock

In the 18th and 19th centuries, some Japanese artists became famous for their "ukiyo-e" paintings and woodblock prints. *Ukiyo-e* means "pictures of the floating world," and most of these were created as woodblock prints, made by carving multiple blocks of wood, then applying ink or colors to them, and then pressing paper on to this to produce prints.

Noboto at Shimōsa (*Shimōsa Noboto*), from the series One Thousand Pictures of the Sea (*Chie no umi*)

Katsushika Hokusai (Japanese), 1832–1833

Around 1833, Hokusai started his series 1,000 Pictures of Ocean and Waterside, but he ended up only making ten prints for it. In each of these, he showed ways that the Japanese people used the sea around them. This shows people digging for shellfish along the shore. There is one boat on the sea and a village across the bay.

Japanese Fashion and Style

From 1603–1868, Japan experienced a peaceful period. During this time, elegant clothes were worn by the rich. *Kosodes* and kimonos, or wrapped garments, were worn to show a person's power and importance. Fabrics were dyed in several colors, and the clothes were often intricately embroidered.

Robe (*Kosode*) with Shells and Sea Grasses

Japan, early 17th century

Like the kimono, a *kosode* is a garment that wraps around the body, but it has fairly narrow sleeves. This *kosode* is printed with scenery from Japan's coast, with beaches scattered with shells and sand. On top of the light blue, the robe is decorated with touches of gold-leaf.

Silk

The finest Japanese clothes were made with silk. Silk fabric was first created in China before 3000 BCE. It was eventually traded across the world. Valuable and expensive silk thread is made by spinning together the silken strands that silkworms produce when wrapping themselves inside a cocoon. To harvest the strands, people put the cocoons in hot water so the silk can be unwound.

Over Robe (Uchikake) with Long-Tailed Birds in a Landscape

Japan, second half 18th century

A *uchikake* is a kind of kimono that is often embellished and worn over a *kosode* as a sort of coat. This *uchikake* is decorated with pictures of birds with long tails, waterfalls, rocks, pine trees, and cherry blossoms. Brightly colored, it is also embroidered with shiny gold thread.

Kabuki Actor Nakamura Tomijuro the First in a Role as a Woman

Katsukawa Shunkō (Japanese), probably 1777

Nakamura Tomijuro was a Japanese actor in the 18th century. At that time, women were not allowed to act on stage, and one of Nakamura's talents was playing female roles. This woodblock print shows Nakamura playing a female character.

Beauty of the Kanbun Era

Japan, late 17th century

Paintings from the late 17th century in Japan of women against a neutral background are often called *Kanbun bijin*, or "Beauty of the Kanbun Era." This woman wears her hair in a fancy style that was called *gosho-mage*, or "palace chignon." She wears a *kosode* with flower patterns, and the patterns of her undergarments can be seen too. Her sash is called an *obi*.

Zodiac Figures

According to the Chinese zodiac, people born in a particular year inherit certain characteristics, represented by animals. These animals include the rat, ox, tiger, rabbit, dragon, snake, horse, ram or goat, monkey, rooster, dog, and pig.

Six of the Twelve Divine Generals
Japan, early 14th century

In East Asian Buddhism, there are 12 protective gods, known as the Twelve Divine Generals. Each general protects and heals certain parts of the body, and Buddhists call on them when they are needed. Here they are, in their fancy armor, with fierce faces, and ready to fight to protect humans. They are sometimes linked with the 12 animals of the Chinese zodiac; here, a zodiac figure is shown in each general's headdress.

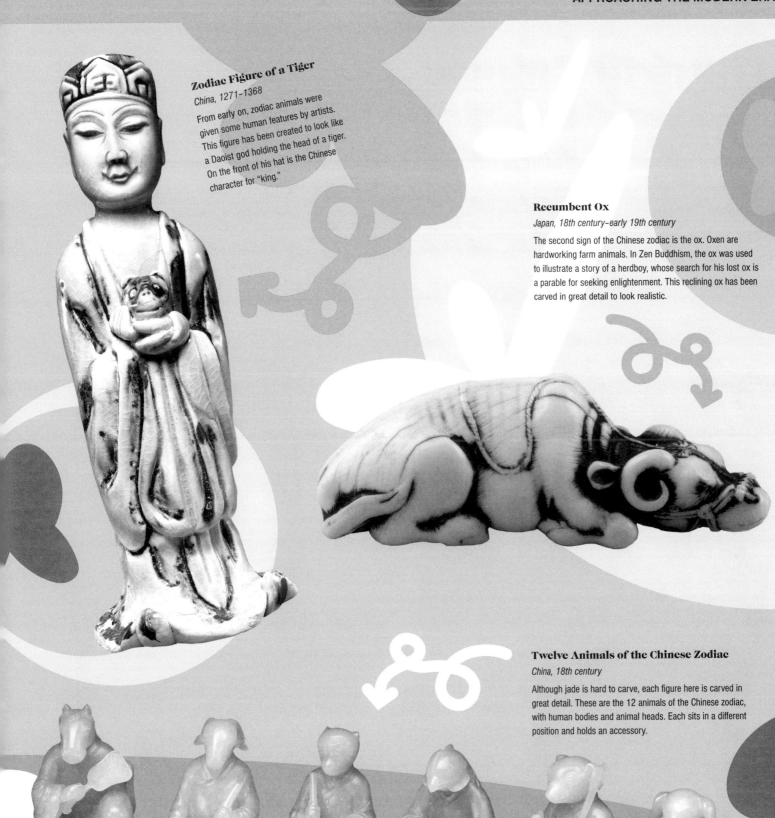

Zodiac Figure of a Tiger

China, 1271–1368

From early on, zodiac animals were given some human features by artists. This figure has been created to look like a Daoist god holding the head of a tiger. On the front of his hat is the Chinese character for "king."

Recumbent Ox

Japan, 18th century–early 19th century

The second sign of the Chinese zodiac is the ox. Oxen are hardworking farm animals. In Zen Buddhism, the ox was used to illustrate a story of a herdboy, whose search for his lost ox is a parable for seeking enlightenment. This reclining ox has been carved in great detail to look realistic.

Twelve Animals of the Chinese Zodiac

China, 18th century

Although jade is hard to carve, each figure here is carved in great detail. These are the 12 animals of the Chinese zodiac, with human bodies and animal heads. Each sits in a different position and holds an accessory.

Timurid Empire

The last great dynasty (family) to rule a huge area in Central Asia was the Timurids. They ruled from about 1307–1507, and their strongest period was during the 15th century. The Timurids built their capital city in Samarqand, Uzbekistan. They valued science, math, literature, and art. They undertook vast building projects and revived learning.

Did you know?

The founder (first ruler) of the Timurid dynasty, Timur, brought artists and craftspeople to Samarqand from different lands that had been conquered by his soldiers. This started one of the most dazzling periods in Islamic art.

Anthology of Persian Poetry

Iran, 15th century

Created during the rule of the grandson of Timur, this hand-painted book features several paintings illustrating poetry.

Qur'an of Ibrahim Sultan

Calligrapher: Ibrahim Sultan (Iranian), AH 830/1427 CE

Ibrahim Sultan was Timur's grandson. He was a patron of the arts and was also a skillful calligrapher. He wrote this Koran manuscript in an elegant script.

New Styles

One of the largest cities of Central Asia, Samarqand was also on the Silk Road, which was the name for several trade routes connecting the East and West of the world. When the Timurid people lived in Samarqand, they mixed artistic styles of other cultures with their own. New styles emerged that later influenced the art of the Mughal Empire.

Wine Drinking in a Spring Garden

Iran, ca. 1430

Here, a young man offers a cup of wine to a young woman. The depicted figures wear lavish dresses, attesting to the individuals' wealth and social rank. This illustration is made in opaque watercolor and gold on undyed silk.

Art and Architecture

Timurid art included colorful illustrated books, detailed paintings, metalwork, ceramics, and carving, as well as many striking buildings, including palaces, mosques, and shrines.

Bowl

Iran or Central Asia, 15th century

The richest members of Timurid society bought Chinese blue-and-white Ming porcelain, but some Timurid artists made less expensive copies like this.

Tile from a Squinch

Uzbekistan, second half 14th century

This brightly colored, carved tile is curved and detailed and made to decorate the inside of an Islamic building.

The Eavesdropper, Folio 47r from a Haft Paikar (Seven Portraits) of the Khamsa (Quintet) of Nizami of Ganja

Herat, Afghanistan, ca. 1430

This illustration by Maulana Azhar is part of a book filled with stories, all illustrated like this. It is made using ink, opaque watercolor, silver, and gold on paper.

Mughal Dynasty

Art flourished in India during the Mughal Empire, reaching a high point from about 1580-1650 under the reigns of the emperors Akbar, Jahangir, and Shah Jahan, who were great patrons and encouraged artists. Mughal painters created detailed, colorful images showing stories, histories, the natural world, and life at court.

Did you know?

The Mughal Empire was a dynasty that ruled most of northern India from the early 16th century to 1848. The Mughals created a united Indian state, where Hindus and Muslims lived alongside each other. It was one of the most multicultural and richest empires that has ever existed.

The Spy Zambur Brings Mahiya to the City of Tawariq

India, ca. 1570

Hamza was the uncle of the Prophet Muhammad, who traveled the world, spreading the teachings of Islam. This is just one of 1,400 paintings of Hamza's life.

Alexander Visits the Sage Plato in His Mountain Cave

Attributed to Basawan (Indian), 1597–1598

Alexander the Great, a king of an ancient kingdom called Macedon, traveled widely. Wearing his turban, he listens to the wise man Plato.

Persian Influence

A huge amount of beautiful art and architecture was created during the nearly 300 years of the Mughal Empire. Artists decorated handwritten books with patterns and made small, detailed paintings called miniatures. These were influenced by Persian miniature art, as the second Mughal emperor Humayun spent time in Persia (modern-day Iran) and brought two Persian painters, Mir Sayyid Ali and Abdus Samad, back to India with him.

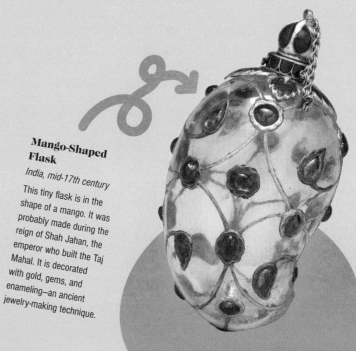

Mango-Shaped Flask

India, mid-17th century

This tiny flask is in the shape of a mango. It was probably made during the reign of Shah Jahan, the emperor who built the Taj Mahal. It is decorated with gold, gems, and enameling—an ancient jewelry-making technique.

Book Painting

Many Mughal paintings were created for handmade books, or manuscripts. Usually several artists, including painters and calligraphers, worked on one book. The *kitabkhana*, or Royal House of Books, was the emperor's library and also where manuscripts were made. Mughal book painting looked unlike any books or art that had been created before. The pictures often showed everyday life in extraordinary settings.

Shah Jahan on Horseback

Payag (Indian), c. 1630

Painted in profile (from the side), the Emperor is on a horse. In grand clothes, he sits on patterned fabrics.

An Old Man and His Young Wife Before Religious Arbitrators

Attributed to Daulat (Indian), 1610–1615

This was probably painted by the Indian artist Daulat, a leading Mughal painter who worked during the reigns of Akbar, Jahangir, and Shah Jahan.

Arjuna Battles Raja Tamradhvaja

India, ca. 1616–1617

Part of a painted manuscript, this was made for a Mughal nobleman who had his own library with other handmade manuscripts.

Buffaloes in Combat

Attributed to Miskin (Indian), late 16th century

Fights between animals, such as buffaloes, were a form of entertainment at the Mughal court. The artist Miskin was a highly skilled animal painter in India at the time.

Safavid Dynasty

From 1501–1722, the great Safavid dynasty controlled a vast area encompassing Iran and parts of Central Asia. The art produced there was often inspired by artists from different regions of the empire and included painted manuscripts, silks, miniatures, ceramics, metal, glass, and lavish architecture.

Most Productive

The Safavid was one of the most important dynasties in Iranian history. Safavid rulers established a particular branch of Shi'a Islam as the official religion of the empire. This contrasted with their neighbors, the Ottoman and Mughal Empires, who followed Sunni Islam. Reflecting Shi'a beliefs, the Safavid period is among the most creative eras of artistic production in Iran.

Did you know?

Artists from different parts of the Safavid Empire were brought together and worked to develop a new Safavid style of painting. Among many things, the artists produced manuscripts using precise lines and details to show stories, myths, battles, local events, and portraits.

Shaikh Mahneh and the Villager
Afghanistan, 1487

This Timurid work depicts a story in which Shaikh Mahneh, a famous nobleman, felt sad. He met a peasant working the land, who glowed with light. The peasant told the Shaikh to be patient.

Silk Animal Carpet
Iran, second half 16th century

In this detailed, closely woven silk carpet, animals including lions, tigers, rams, and dragons fight against a background of flowering plants.

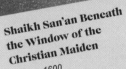

Shaikh San'an Beneath the Window of the Christian Maiden

Iran, ca. 1600

This illustrates a story of Shaikh San'an, who fell in love with a Christian girl and temporarily lost his faith in Islam. Below the balcony, his friends look upset.

Allegory of Worldly and Otherworldly Drunkenness

Sultan Muhammad (Iranian), ca. 1531–1533

Painted by artist Sultan Muhammad, this illustrates verses by the great mystical poet Hafiz. People and angels are intoxicated with wine.

Binding for the Mantiq al-tayr

Iran, ca. 1600

Painted with gold leaf, this is the cover for a handmade book. The format is characteristic of Safavid bindings, with its central medallion and elaborate decorative border.

The Ottoman Empire

Beginning in what is now Turkey around 1300, the Ottoman Empire (ca. 1299–1923) grew to cover a huge area, including parts of the Middle East, Europe, and North Africa. By the 1500s, it was one of the greatest powers in the world. A lot of art was produced for the Ottoman sultan and his court, and artists were brought there from all over the empire.

How Styles Spread

Artists from many different places gathered at the court of the Ottoman sultan, where they exchanged ideas and developed an official court style. Popular motifs developed and were copied throughout the empire.

Did you know?

Various artistic styles became popular at the Ottoman court. One style was called *saz* and included feathery leaves. Another style developed floral motifs including roses, carnations, hyacinths, tulips, and honeysuckles. Sometimes the floral style also featured feathery leaves.

Part of a Valance
Greek, 18th century

Part of the furnishings for a bed or sofa, this detailed embroidery includes turbaned horsemen, servants, birds, animals, flowers, and arches.

Gospel with Silver Cover
Turkey, 13th and 17th century

People of different religions lived in the Turkish world, including Christians and Jews. This is a Christian book cover, with silver and gemstones, showing Bible stories.

Tile Panel with Wavy-Vine Design
Syria, 16th–17th century

Created near Syria, this panel of six tiles includes a repeating pattern of dark-blue grape leaves, curly tendrils, and bunches of grapes.

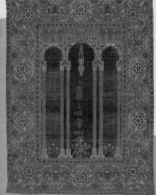

Tughra of Sultan Süleiman the Magnificent
Turkey, ca. 1565–1560

Made using ink, watercolor, and gold on paper, a *tughra* is an insignia or emblem representing an Ottoman sultan.

Carpet with Triple-Arch Design
Turkey, ca. 1575–1590

This carefully woven carpet showing a three-arched gateway and a lamp was probably used as a prayer rug by someone in the Ottoman court.

Fragment of a Kaftan Back
Turkey, mid-16th century

Once part of the back of a kaftan that was worn by the sultan or another important person, this bold design of peacock feathers is made of silk with silver or gold colored threads.

The Aztecs

The Aztecs lived in the valley of Mexico from the 14th to the 16th centuries. They built magnificent cities, including their capital city Tenochtitlán, and they worshiped many gods. They made striking art to express their religious beliefs.

Temple Models

Small models of temples were made in order to encourage people to worship gods at home. This object is part of a temple model and would have been painted in bright colors. Each model depicts key details of the real-life temple.

Temple Model
Aztec, 1400–1521

Kneeling Female Deity
Aztec, 15th–early 16th century

Water Deity (Chalchiuhtlicue)
Aztec, 15th–early 16th century
Chalchiuhtlicue means "She of the Jade Skirt." She is the Aztec goddess of water and the protector of babies.

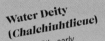

Standard Bearer

Aztec, 15th–early 16th century

Because of how he holds his right hand, this sculpture of a man has been called a "standard bearer." These sorts of sculptures were placed at the top of a temple pyramid, holding a rod tipped with a flag or banner called a standard.

Maize Deity (*Chicomecoátl*)

Aztec, 15th–early 16th century

Chicomecoátl is the name of an Aztec goddess of maize (corn), which was the main food in the Mesoamerican diet. Corn was such an important crop that there were many gods representing its various stages of development. This figure represents ripened corn. She holds a pair of corncobs in each hand and wears a large headdress.

Corn was an important crop to the Aztecs.

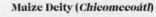

The Inca

The Inca Empire dates to about 1425–1532. Inca artists made polished metalwork, ceramics, and textiles. They were experts at weaving and embroidery, often using fine wool from alpacas and llamas.

Did you know?

The Inca believed there were separate worlds for the gods, the living, and the dead. The worlds were symbolized by three animals. The condor represented the world of the gods, the puma was associated with the world of the living, and the snake was connected to the world of the dead.

Kero
Inca, 15th–early 16th century

Kero
Inca, 16th–18th century

Many Gods

The Inca people believed in multiple gods. The main deities associated with the Inca were Inti, the sun god; Pachamama, the Earth goddess; Killa, the moon goddess; and the Apus, the spirits of the mountains.

Serpent Ornament

Inca, 1450–1532

Historians are not sure exactly what this snake was used for. The heavy head might mean it was used as a weapon, to be swung at enemies. Snakes were symbols of protection.

Feathered Tunic

Inca, 15th–early 16th century

This featherwork garment was painstakingly constructed by sewing brightly colored plumage from tropical birds living in the region onto a cotton base, feather by feather. Featherworks were worn by royalty or during rituals and may have also been associated with the Inca military.

Female Figurine

Inca, 1400–1533

This statue of a standing woman with a large head was probably used in sacred rituals.

Male Figurine

Inca, 1400–1533

A man wearing a *llautu*, an Inca headdress, was an Inca sacred being. He may have been offered to Inca gods in worship.

Gold Paintings in Italy

Paintings in Italy from the 1300s often featured figures or stories from Christianity. In religious art, gold represented Heaven and the light of God. As the paintings were often seen by candlelight, the gold appeared to glow and shimmer in a mystical way. Artists used gold leaf to create this effect. Gold leaf was the most expensive pigment, so paintings that used it were particularly precious.

Did you know?

Gold leaf is used in lots of kinds of art throughout history and around the world. It is used in Buddhist art for decorating statues and symbols, and in Islamic calligraphy and manuscript illumination. It is made by hammering gold (the softest metal) into incredibly thin sheets. This process is called *goldbeating*.

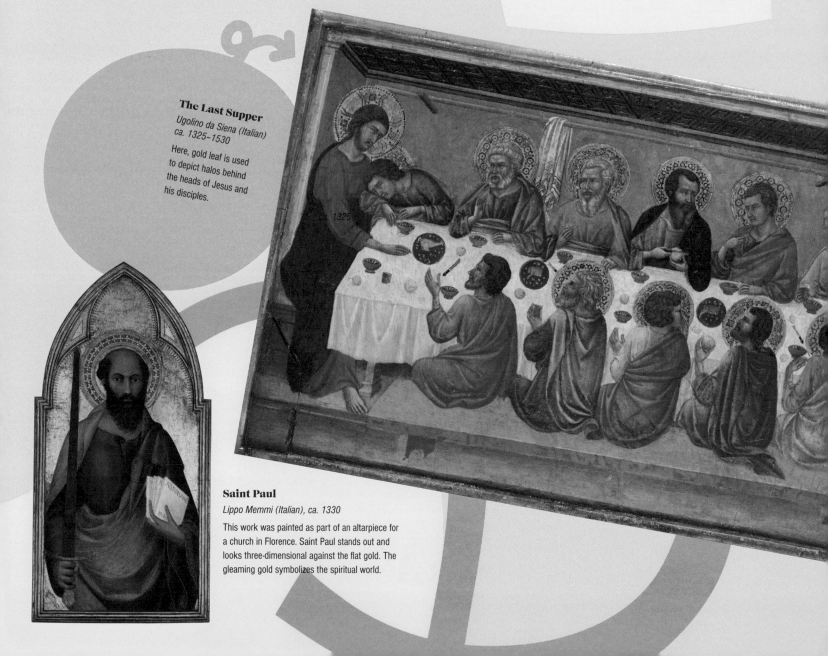

The Last Supper
Ugolino da Siena (Italian) ca. 1325–1530

Here, gold leaf is used to depict halos behind the heads of Jesus and his disciples.

Saint Paul

Lippo Memmi (Italian), ca. 1330

This work was painted as part of an altarpiece for a church in Florence. Saint Paul stands out and looks three-dimensional against the flat gold. The gleaming gold symbolizes the spiritual world.

David

Lorenzo Monaco (Italian), ca. 1408–1410

In the Old Testament, David was a prophet and a king. Here, he has been painted by Lorenzo Monaco, who was the leading painter in Florence. Sitting on a stone seat set against a gold background, David wears a green cloak lined with pink and a crown. He holds a stringed instrument.

Saint Anthony of Padua

Maso di Banco (Italian), ca. 1340

This is the Portuguese Saint Anthony of Padua. He was usually shown holding a book as a sign of his learning. The way he is painted here makes it seem as though he is looking out of the painting at something else. This painting was made to be displayed in a church. Originally, the Virgin Mary and Jesus would have been in a center panel next to Saint Anthony.

The Adoration of the Magi

Giotto di Bondone (Italian), ca. 1320

This painting by Giotto di Bondone shows the stable where Jesus was born. One of the kneeling Magi, or wise men, picks up Jesus as Mary looks on, concerned. Giotto was one of the first Western artists to portray human emotions and to make art seem lifelike. The painting shows an unfolding story: in the front, the three Magi are worshiping the baby, while in the background, an angel announces the birth of Jesus to two shepherds.

New Subjects

During the Renaissance in Italy, which flourished in Venice, Florence, and Rome in the 15th and 16th centuries, artists looked to history and poetry, and especially to the stories of Greece and Rome, to find inspiration for their work. These nonreligious subjects reflected the interests of Humanists, scholars who were interested in studying human existence and reviving the classical past. Many of these people also commissioned portraits that celebrated their intellect and status.

Making it Real

Paolo Veronese was an important 16th-century painter in Venice. In the painting on the left, he depicts an ancient Roman story, making it look as if it were happening during his own time. Mars wears a suit of armor, and Venus wears the jewels of a noblewoman in Venice. Veronese's skill in painting textures and colors realistically made him famous across Italy.

Mars and Venus United by Love
Paolo Veronese (Italian), 1570s
In ancient Rome, Mars was the god of war, and Venus the goddess of love. Here, with Cupid, they embrace—showing how love makes everything better.

Portrait of a Young Man
Bronzino (Italian), 1530s

It is not known who this young man is, but he would have been an important figure in his day.

Portrait of a Woman with a Man at a Casement
Fra Filippo Lippi (Italian), ca. 1440

This woman faces a window where a man appears—possibly her future husband.

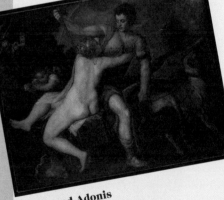

Venus and Adonis
Titian (Italian), 1550s

One of the most important painters in Venice, Titian was known for his colorful paintings filled with textures, movement, and emotions.

A Sense of Movement

Among the new ideas for subjects, artists painted—or sculpted—figures looking as if they were moving. You can see opposite that Venus and Mars are chatting with little Cupid, and the four musicians (right) are all busy doing things.

The Musicians
Caravaggio (Italian), 1597

Spanish Painting

From the late 16th to the early 19th centuries, Spanish art was often dramatic. Artists at this time included El Greco, Jusepe de Ribera, Diego Velázquez, and Francisco de Goya. They painted or sculpted histories, important people, landscapes, Christian subjects, and still lifes. They made them look natural and realistic, often copying aspects of everyday life.

Juan de Pareja
Diego Velázquez (Spanish), 1650

The Spanish king's favorite painter, Velázquez, painted this portrait of his assistant, Juan de Pareja. At the time this was painted, Juan de Pareja was an enslaved man. He later gained his freedom and became a painter himself.

Majas on a Balcony
Attributed to Goya (Spanish), ca. 1800–1810

Probably painted by Francisco de Goya, here are two women on a balcony with two guards in the shadows behind them.

The Holy Family with Saints Anne and Catherine of Alexandria
Jusepe de Ribera (Spanish), 1648

This was painted from real models posing to depict people from the Bible. It uses strong light effects to create a vivid scene.

Drama and Contrast

Spanish artists were influenced by the Italian Renaissance, and because the Church was the main patron of the arts, a lot of it was about Christianity. But Spanish artists also concentrated on different subject matter, including still lifes and landscapes, using dark shadows for drama and contrast.

View of Toledo
*El Greco (Greek),
ca. 1599–1600*

In his dramatic dark style, El Greco painted the city he loved, Toledo, from various views at once, not what it looked like from one angle.

The Afternoon Meal (*La Merienda*)

*Luis Meléndez (Spanish),
ca. 1772*

Meléndez painted a realistic still life against a sunny landscape. This scene shows the artist's astonishing painting skills.

Virgin and Child

Bartolomé Esteban Murillo (Spanish), 1670s

Murillo often painted the Virgin and Child, using soft shadows and lifelike poses to make them seem sweet, realistic, and close.

Flanders

From the 15th to the 17th centuries, the region of Flanders, in the modern country of Belgium, was one of the wealthiest artistic centers in Europe. While the Northern Netherlands broke away from Spanish rule and became officially Protestant in the late 16th century, this region remained a part of the Spanish empire with a largely Catholic population.

The Holy Family with Saint Elizabeth, Saint John, and a Dove
Peter Paul Rubens (Flemish), ca. 1608–1609

This was probably painted soon after Peter Paul Rubens returned to Antwerp, in Flanders, from Rome, in Italy, where he had become a leading artist. The dove symbolizes the Holy Spirit.

Color and Texture

Flemish painters were experts in using oil paints, creating brilliantly colored, lifelike images, often to do with the Catholic faith and influenced by Italian art. They created drama and rhythm in their paintings.

The Nativity
Workshop of Rogier van der Weyden (Netherlandish), mid-15th century

Painted by the influential Rogier van der Weyden and his workshop, this altarpiece shows the Bible story of the Nativity.

The Annunciation
Gerard David (Netherlandish),1506
Commissioned by a rich Italian banker, these panels were painted by Gerard David for an altar in a church in Italy. The altarpiece was meant to be viewed from below.

Making it Real

Flemish artists were mainly Catholic; therefore, a lot of their work was for churches. They used oils to paint realistically, with plenty of details and textures. They also aimed to make their paintings seem real to viewers, so they often set them in what looked like ordinary homes.

Self-Portrait
Anthony Van Dyck (Flemish), ca. 1620–1621
The artist Anthony Van Dyck has painted himself as an aristocrat, not a painter. Artists often painted self-portraits to show off their skills.

The Annunciation
Hans Memling (Netherlandish), ca. 1465–1470
The Annunciation, when the Virgin Mary learned from the angel Gabriel that she was pregnant with the Christ Child, was a popular story for Catholic painters. Flemish artists sometimes painted Bible stories as if they were happening inside homes.

Portrait of a Man
Hugo van der Goes (Netherlandish), ca. 1475
Flemish artists became known for their lifelike paintings. Hugo van der Goes painted a realistic portrait of a man in strong light and shade.

Woodcuts and Printing

The Protestant Reformation in some parts of Germany meant that there was less demand for large religious art in churches. So, many German artists made smaller works, often for private worship, including prints that sold well, often woodcuts or etchings. The most famous printmaker was Albrecht Dürer.

Strong Contrasts

Having spent time in Italy, Albrecht Dürer became well known for mixing Italian and German art ideas. German artists picked up some of these ideas, such as making their art more natural, but they also used particularly strong contrasts of color or tone.

Landscape with a Double Spruce

Albrecht Altdorfer (German), ca. 1521–1522

This landscape of a German valley has been created with etching, which is when the artist uses acid to burn into a metal plate, and ink to create the picture.

Adam and Eve
Albrecht Dürer (German), 1504

Dürer shows his thinking about perfect human proportions (measurements) in this engraving.

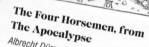

The Four Horsemen, from The Apocalypse
Albrecht Dürer (German), 1498

This woodcut print by Dürer shows part of a story from the Bible. Dürer makes the story seem lively and powerful.

The Witches
Hans Baldung Grien (German), 1510

Some German artists became extremely skilled in creating prints with details and strong light and dark tones. This depicts three witches around a cauldron. The gray ink enhances the dark subject matter.

Printing Books

In 1450, in Germany, Johannes Gutenberg invented the printing press. It changed the world. Before that, books were made slowly and expensively by hand, but suddenly, thousands of books could be made cheaply. This meant that for the first time, many people could buy books, so they could learn, pass on information, and share discoveries.

Melancolia I
Albrecht Dürer (German), 1514

Full of mysteries, this engraving by Dürer is generally believed to represent Dürer's own personality. The winged woman depicts his idea of "melancolia," or *melancholy*, which means "sadness."

Britain

During the 18th and 19th centuries, in Britain, the Industrial Revolution was making many lives easier, but also a lot of other lives harder. Many lost their jobs as machines did their work for them, and a number of rich people grew richer while the poor became poorer. British artists became particularly famed for their portrait and landscape paintings and depictions of stories.

Did you know?

In the 19th century, artists explored new ways of painting and formed art groups. These included the Pre-Raphaelite Brotherhood, which was a secret to begin with. Another group of artists worked in Scotland and was called The Glasgow School.

The Love Song

Sir Edward Burne-Jones (British), 1868–1877

Sir Edward Burne-Jones painted this when thinking about a French folk song. He was trying to capture a look of the past.

Popularity

Landscape painting reminded viewers of the journeys they took on the new railways across Britain and Europe, and portraits included paintings of people and favorite animals and pets, which made the subjects look noble. Artists such as William Blake, J. M. W. Turner, John Constable, Dante Gabriel Rossetti, and John-Everett Millais became sought after.

The Lake of Zug

J. M. W. Turner (British), 1843

Joseph Mallord William Turner was one of the greatest landscape painters—he changed history with his exciting watercolor and oil paintings.

Lady Lilith
Dante Gabriel Rossetti (British), 1867

Dante Gabriel Rossetti, one of the Pre-Raphaelite Brotherhood, painted this lady from a story. The flowers symbolize different kinds of love.

The Third Duke of Dorset's Hunter with a Groom and a Dog
George Stubbs (British), 1768

George Stubbs was the greatest painter of animal portraits of his time. This shows a rich duke's horse, groom, and dog.

Wooded Upland Landscape
Thomas Gainsborough (British), ca. 1783

Although Thomas Gainsborough made many drawings from real landscapes, this is from his imagination.

Salisbury Cathedral from the Bishop's Grounds
John Constable (British), ca. 1825

John Constable liked to paint large landscapes of places he loved. With their lively brushwork, his large sketches for finished paintings were revolutionary at the time.

Captain George K. H. Coussmaker (1759–1801)
Sir Joshua Reynolds (British), 1782

Virgil's Tomb by Moonlight, with Silius Italicus Declaiming
Joseph Wright (Wright of Derby) (British), 1779

British artist Joseph Wright depicts a place in Naples. Many wealthy viewers in London would recognize it from the Grand Tour.

The Fortune-Teller

Georges de La Tour (French), ca. 1630s

Georges de La Tour was an expert in creating stories in paintings. Here, a woman reads a young man's fortune as her friends rob him.

France

In France in the 17th century, the Royal Academy of Painting and Sculpture was created, which was a powerful institution that controlled French art for more than 200 years. French art from that time until the 19th century dominated the world, and many new art styles began there. Most of the artists here were members of the academy.

The Fortune-Teller

Georges de La Tour (French), ca. 1630s

Georges de La Tour was an expert in creating stories in paintings. Here, a woman reads a young man's fortune as her friends rob him.

The Stolen Kiss

Jean-Honoré Fragonard (French), ca. 1760

Rococo art was light-hearted. Jean-Honoré Fragonard painted fun events, with people wearing elegant clothes and enjoying life.

**Saints Peter and John
Healing the Lame Man**
Nicolas Poussin (French), 1655

Influenced by Italian Renaissance painters,
Nicolas Poussin paints a Bible story. Two
of Christ's apostles cure a man who could
not walk.

Mezzetin
Antoine Watteau (French), ca. 1718–1720

Soap Bubbles
Jean Siméon Chardin (French), ca. 1733–34

Inspired by 17th-century painters from the
Netherlands, Jean Siméon Chardin painted people
from ordinary life, looking natural.

Revolution!

From 1789 to 1799, the
French Revolution occurred.
The people overthrew the
monarchy and took control
of the government. Several
artists painted through this
time, including Jacques-
Louis David. An art style
called Neoclassicism
that looks polished and
smooth emerged.

The Third-Class Carriage
Honoré Daumier (French), ca. 1862–1864

The Death of Socrates
Jacques-Louis David (French), ca. 1787

Catching a Scene

From the 17th century, French art began to be noticed more than Italian or Netherlandish art for the first time in centuries. Many young French painters went to Rome to study art. On their return to France, although they were influenced by Italy, they developed their own styles and techniques. Among their ideas, they made landscapes and light especially important.

Did you know?

Before the late 19th century, art—especially in France—had strict rules. Painting was ranked in order of what was generally thought to be important. So, paintings of history, the Bible, or other subjects with lots of people were the most important, then portraits, then landscapes, and finally still lifes.

Hagar in the Wilderness
Camille Corot (French), 1835

This scene tells a Bible story about the family of Abraham. It was painted by Camille Corot, who painted in front of a real landscape.

The Importance of Landscape

Although landscape painting had been important in Asia for centuries, in the West, landscapes were usually only painted as backgrounds for human activity. By the 18th and 19th centuries, many European artists made landscape painting important. In France, several painters captured the scenery and light, using small brush marks and bold colors.

View of Ornans
Gustave Courbet (French), probably mid-1850s

Gustave Courbet painted this of his home town. Look down and across the river to see the church steeple and cluster of houses.

Landscape with a Sunlit Stream
Charles-François Daubigny (French), ca. 1877

Charles-François Daubigny captured scenes in the countryside. He floated on his studio-boat and painted with flicks of his brush.

Pastoral Landscape: The Roman Campagna
Claude Lorrain (French), ca. 1639

The landscape artist Claude Lorrain inspired many others with his paintings filled with golden light, shadows, and often ancient buildings too.

Painting Outside

Artists such as Claude Monet, some Netherlandish painters, and English painters Turner and Constable made landscape painting important. In the 19th century, some French artists began painting outside in front of their chosen landscapes, trying to capture the scenes as naturally as possible. Many of them focused on capturing the light and creating many different greens, using quick brushstrokes and appealing arrangements.

Vessels

These pages explore tableware made from about 4000 BCE to the early 20th century, from the red- and black-figure pottery made in the workshops of ancient Athens in Greece to the silver Samuel Casey creampot from the United States. Across thousands of years, expert makers used the jugs and vases that decorate our tables to display skills in ceramics, glassmaking, and metalworking, creating vessels to store wine, serve food, or simply create a brilliant display.

Terracotta Kylix (drinking cup)
Greek, 6th century BCE

1. Exekias, Black-Figure Neck-Amphora with Lid, Greece, Attributed to Exekias (Greek), ca. 540 BCE **2.** Goblet, Venice, ca. 1475 **3.** Bowl with Three Dragons, China, 10th century **4.** Cup with Four Gazelles, Iran, ca. 1000–800 BCE **5.** Joseph Smith Pottery, Pennsylvania, ca. 1769 **6.** Luster Bowl with Winged Horse, Iran, late 12th century **7.** Ewer with a Feline-Shaped Handle, Iran, 7th century **8.** Beaker with Birds and Animals, Thrace, ca. 400–300 BCE **9.** Covered Beaker, Italy, ca. 1325–1350 (vessel); Austria, ca. 1340–1360 (mounts) **10.** American Flint Glass Manufactory, Pocket Bottle, America, 1769–1774 **11.** Beaker with Apes, South Netherlands, ca. 1425–1450 **12.** Ewer, China, 11th–12th century **13.** Oil Jug (*lekythos*), Greece, ca. 550 BCE **14.** Jug, Great Britain, early–mid-16th century **15.** Plate with the Battle of David and Goliath, Byzantium, ca. 629–630 **16.** Ewer, France, ca. 1550 **17.** Flask, China, ca. 9th century **18.** Pierced Jug with Harpies and Sphinxes, Iran, 1215/16 **19.** Pair of Skyphoi with Relief Decoration, Rome, early 1st century BCE **20.** Samuel Casey Creampot, America, 1750–1770

Portraits of Kingship

The Edo people believe that your soul or life force is concentrated in your head. When creating a sculpture to celebrate the life of the Oba—the title of the king of Benin—they are not creating a portrait but rather reflecting on an ideal of beauty and the ruler's inner self and wisdom in the sculpture's features. For example, a large forehead represents that the individual was very wise. Often placed on altars after the death of the king, they are a way to honor the former ruler and allow people to leave offerings and commune with the Oba's spirit.

Portrait of a leader

The leaders or Obas in the Benin Kingdom trace the history of their ruling dynasty back to the 14th century. The role of Oba has been, and still is, passed down from father to firstborn son. The Heads of the Oba are not meant to be actual portraits but represent an idealized version of the king.

Head of an Oba
Edo peoples, 16th century

The woven headdress that hangs down from the side of the Oba's head and the necklaces around his neck signify that he is king. Although they are depicted here in brass, in real life, this crown and related finery are made from bright-red coral. Coral is a material that can only be worn by the Oba, his family, or other high-ruling officials. Because it comes from the ocean, but can also exist outside the ocean, it represents the Oba's ability to exist in the earthly world as well as in the spiritual one.

Head of an Oba
Edo peoples, 1550–1680

The material used to make this head and the others on this page is brass. Brass was important for these sculptures because it was considered a precious material and a marker of wealth. Also celebrated for its shininess, brass is understood as having the potential to deflect evil.

Head of an Oba
Edo peoples, 17th century

The Edo people believe that the head is the center for someone's inner self, such as knowledge, leadership, and ancestry. This was even more important for the Oba, who is considered "The Great Head," because it is his head that leads the kingdom, oversees religious events, and rules over daily life. Even from the side, we can see that the head of the Oba is depicted in a scale that is larger than life-sized, but with sharp and defined features.

Did you know?

The first job for the new king would be to commission a bronze sculptural head of the previous king, his father. This head would then be placed in a shrine set up to honor the new Oba's predecessor. Placed in the shrine, along with other objects of power, the Head of the Oba became a vessel through which kings could transfer their power to their successors. Even though his father was no longer there to guide him, the king could go to the altar as a way to connect with his father. The Oba's sculptures also served as a reminder of ancestry. The ruler would have portraits of his father, grandfather, great-grandfather, and even further back for hundreds of years!

Head of an Oba
Edo peoples, 18th century

Artists established a standardized pattern of representation for the Obas, such as the large head and wide eyes. This gave the heads a consistent family resemblance, similar to a series of family photographs. While they share many similarities, there are some unique aspects to each face. Compared to the others on these pages, this Oba's face has very large eyes but a smaller mouth. This shows there were differences between how each Oba wanted themselves to be depicted.

Head of an Oba
Edo peoples, 19th century

Kings of Benin wore lattice-patterned coral crowns that hung down on either side of the Oba's face. While the designs started off simple, over time, they became more elaborate, like in this example, to signify the rising status of the Oba as the leader of the powerful kingdom of Benin. This example has an elaborate headdress of latticed coral and additional adornments on his crown. The emphasis on coral shows the Oba's wealth and also control over the industries of trade.

Ere Ibeji Twin Figures

The Yoruba people of West Africa have the highest incidence of twin births not only in Nigeria but in the world. In Yoruba culture, twins are understood to have special spiritual advantages in life and to possess spiritual powers. They are protected by the Yoruba god, also known as an *orisha*, named Shango, the god of thunder. If one twin dies, a small sculpture is made of them to honor them. This small sculpture is not a portrait of the deceased twin but rather a physical space where their spirit can be made present.

Did you know?

In Yoruba, twins are referred to as *ere ibeji*. *Ere* means "sacred," *ibi* means "born," and *eji* means "two." The power of twins is further also understood through their birth order. It is understood that the first twin to be born is the watcher. They come into the world first to judge that it is adequate for the second twin, who is considered the wiser, elder of the two to be born.

Twin Figure: Male (*Ibeji*)
Yoruba, 19th–20th century

With the god of thunder, Shango, as their protector, twins are believed to be able to bestow good fortune on their family and misfortune on anyone who does not honor them, both in life and death. The small pendant around this figure's neck may be a protective amulet or an offering to celebrate the *ibeji*'s spirit.

Twin Figure: Male with Garment (*Ewu ileke Ibeji*)
Yoruba, 19th–20th century

In this sculpture, you can see the twin figure wearing a garment made of cowrie shells. Cowrie shells were traditionally used as a form of money, so placing an outfit made of that object onto an *ibeji* is a reference to wealth and honor.

Twin Figure: Female (*Ibeji*)

Yoruba, 19th-20th century

Twin figures, like this one, are represented in a state of adulthood, with mature adult features and often elaborate hairstyles.

Twin Figure: Male (*Ibeji*)

Yoruba, 19th-20th century

The family takes daily care of the twin figure. The daily handling and care given to the twin figure by the family can give it a distinctive shiny patina, or surface. Once the surviving twin reaches adulthood, they take over the daily responsibilities of care.

Twin Figure: Female (*Ibeji*)

Yoruba, 19th-20th century

The sculpture or sculptures of the deceased twin are treated as a physical object that the spirit of the deceased twin can inhabit. The entire family, particularly the mother, treats the twin figure as if it is a living person. The *ibeji* statue will be bathed, fed, dressed with clothes, and adorned with accessories, like the ones shown here.

The Power of Twins

If one or both twins die and are not properly honored, this can mean misfortune for their parents as well as their community. To counteract this, the parents will meet with a diviner—someone who can communicate with the spiritual world—to make a small, portable sculpture of the deceased twin or twins to continue to honor their spirit. The diviner communes with the spirit to ensure that the physical statue is aesthetically pleasing to the spirit and shows the twin in a perpetual state of idealized adulthood. While these *ere ibeji* are hand carved, today they are mass produced, often out of plastic, and can be bought at many stores in Nigeria.

Seeing Privacy

The Dogon people of Mali live in a plateau region. Dominated by the Bandiagara Escarpment, a 1,600-ft-tall (500-m) sandstone cliff, the Dogon people carve their homes, temples, and other sacred spaces into the steep cliffs. They are an agricultural society, meaning that their economy is based on farming the land. The majority of Dogon works are understood to deal with fertility, both of the Dogon land and people. Many of the works on this page were intended to be placed in private spaces.

Front

Back

Seated Couple
Dogon peoples, 18th–early 19th century

This well-known piece shows a man and woman sharing a seat, with the male figure's arms framing them. Their bodies mirror one another as they embrace, making them appear as one. Although they are depicted as a unit, the back of each figure has details that show the roles they each play in society. On the back of the man is a quiver of arrows, and on the woman's back is a small baby. The objects are also a subtle reminder of fertility.

Dry Climate

The very little rainfall near the Sahara Desert results in a very dry climate. Combined with the shelter the escarpment provides, this means that many Dogon works are incredibly well preserved. In such a dry climate, rain is vital to maintaining the agricultural society of the Dogon people. Droughts are something that the Dogon people deal with frequently. The figure shown on the right here is raising his hands, to show him connecting Heaven and Earth. He is doing this so that he can communicate with ancestral spirits to appeal for good rainfall.

Male Figure with Raised Arms
Dogon peoples, 17th–19th century

This work was carved hundreds of years ago. One of the largest Dogon sculptures, this object was made for a shrine carved into the escarpment. The figure's stylized beard, belt, anklets and armlets, and neck pendant signify that he is an elder who may have been a priest.

Ring: Equestrian Figure
Dogon peoples, 19th–20th century

This copper-alloy ring was made using the "lost wax" method, in which a mold is created using wax, which is then melted and drained away.

Private Objects

Many of the objects on these two pages, like the Figure with Raised Arms and Female Figures, were intended to be seen primarily by the extended family that originally owned them. Museums are public settings in which many such historical art forms that were once private become accessible to all. If these objects were only intended to be seen by community members, but are now on display in a museum, should we be looking at them? How does viewing them out of context change how we experience and understand them?

While we are looking at these works as important examples of what other cultures created, we can learn about the beliefs and customs they relate to. Like most religious art in museums, the artists were creating a figure that could hold the spirit of an ancestor and be a place where the earthly and spiritual realms could meet. While we recognize their power as works of art, these objects were not simply created to be displayed but were the focus of prayers directed at family altars in the Dogon people's villages.

Because these objects are places where a spirit can physically exist, do ancestral spirits still inhabit them? If so, what different role do they now play in a museum?

Lidded Vessel: Equestrian Figure

Dogon peoples, 16th–early 20th century

Altar: Female Figures

Dogon peoples, 16th–early 20th century

Like the Figure with Raised Arms, which was made for a private altarpiece in a shrine, the three objects pictured on this page were made for private purposes. The exact purpose of the works is not well understood. However, this one on the right is thought to have been created as a site of communication with the ancestors.

Figure: Pair of Balafon Players

Dogon peoples, 18th–early 19th century

Sacred Stools

Within many different African societies, stools are very important for a society's leader or king. As symbolic seats, they are not actually used as ordinary chairs. They are not sat on by anyone but function as a seat for the soul of the stool's owner. The stools are incredibly powerful royal objects. They serve almost as a photograph of the ruler, as a way to remember and honor them in life and death. For the Akan people, when a king or Oba dies, they use an Akan phrase that translates to "the stool has fallen" to alert the community to their leader's passing.

Seat of the Soul

Seen as a connection between the earthly world and the spiritual world, the soul of the king is just as important as his physical body, and so it gets its own seat. In many societies, even after death, the king's stool is seen as a site where his soul resides and where people can come to make offerings to the deceased king. In many African societies, the stools are so important that they often have never actually touched the floor and are protected from public view.

Royal Seat

Akan Peoples, 19th–20th century

For the Akan people, their connection to stools is part of their empire's history. Legend says that their first king, a man named Osei Tutu, was sitting under a tree in the early 1700s when a stool fell from the sky into his lap. He took this as a physical and metaphorical sign that the Akan gods supported his rule.

Female Power

In some African cultures, women's bodies are depicted as holding up the seat of the stool, often on the tips of their fingers. The position of women in society is important. For many societies, like the Luba, while the ruler is male, and leadership is passed down through the father's line, leadership is still symbolized by images of women. It is the female body that gives birth to kings and raises the future leader. Women take care of others and serve as female priestesses within religious contexts. For the Luba people, upon the death of a king, an older woman is tasked with holding his soul within her body. The stylized female body supporting the seat of the stool reflects the fact that the work women do supports their societies in more ways than one. The royal seats pay homage to the king and how his influence will be maintained in this life and the next.

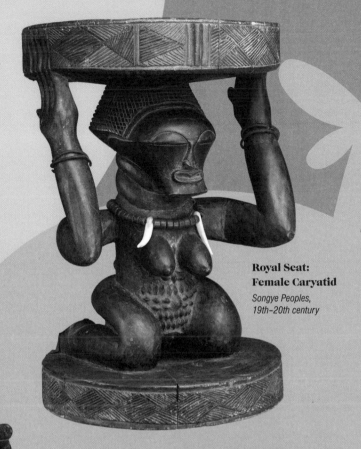

**Royal Seat:
Female Caryatid**
*Songye Peoples,
19th–20th century*

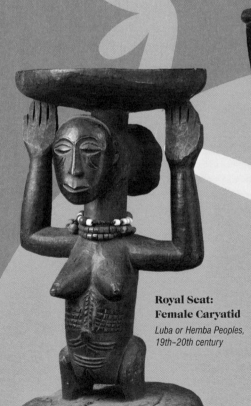

**Royal Seat:
Female Caryatid**
*Luba or Hemba Peoples,
19th–20th century*

**Royal Seat (Lupona):
Female Caryatid**
*Luba or Hemba Peoples,
19th century*

**Royal Seat: Leopards
and Female Figures**
Noni Peoples, 19th–20th century

This stool shows female figures sitting on top of leopards. The leopard is a symbol of the king's power in African cultures because of its courage, stealth, and bravery. Combining the mothers of kings sitting atop the animal representation of a king to support the seat for his soul shows the power between the two.

Tracking History

On these pages, we are going to explore how different African cultural groups keep track of their personal and cultural histories. These objects may look different from the record-keeping objects you may be familiar with, such as books, documents, and file cabinets, but for some African cultural groups, these objects function in a similar way. For many African cultural groups, history is not written down but passed down through shared stories. Visual devices like these help people remember these histories and cultural stories.

Did you know?

Similar to a filing system, each of the nails in this *Nkisi N'Kondi* represents a vow, law, or commitment made between two people. The person who knew the history and backstory of each nail and the law or vow it signified was known as a *nganga*. The *nganga* were important members of Congo society. The position was hereditarily passed down and was part of an oral tradition of record keeping. The nails were the physical object of memory, and a learned history of their positions would allow the *nganga* to recall the memories associated with each one.

Memory Board (*Lukasa*)
Luba Peoples, 19th–20th century

The Luba people used *Lukasas*, or memory boards, to keep track of important historical events. These handheld objects are made of wood and are physical representations of spiritual ideas. Diviners use mounds of wood often adorned with shells and beads to communicate to the Luba people's history keepers.

Mangaaka Power Figure (*Nkisi N'Kondi*)
Kongo artist and nganga, *Yombe group, second half of the 19th century*

This *Nkisi N'Kondi* is a male figure with nails sticking out of his body. He is a representation of enforcing the vows, laws, and treatises that the object records.

Plaque: Warrior and Attendants

Edo peoples, 16th–17th century

While the specific historical moment that this object represents has been lost, we know that this plaque shows a moment when an important warrior is either headed to or returning from war, surrounded by his attendants.

Storytelling

Each of the objects on this spread represents a different way to remember a story or a history. Luba memory boards use visual designs, such as a carving of a chief's face, to remind the user of the history the board documents. The Edo plaque of a Warrior and Attendants documents a particular moment from the Edo people's history, like a photograph. Immortalized in bronze, this important moment is part of a visual history. The Akan linguist staff references an Akan proverb using the image of a spiderweb.

Figurative Harp (*Domu*)

Mangbetu Peoples, 19th–20th century

While no longer made in Mangbetu society, harps like this one combine the body of a musical instrument with a neck adorned with the head of a person. Celebrated for their artistic quality, these harps would also have been used to play songs telling Mangbetu oral histories and stories. The harp's owner would also perform songs about their experiences.

Staff of Office: Figures, Spider Web, and Spider Motif

Akan Peoples, 19th–early 20th century

Linguists were important people who worked as translators and diplomats. They were also keepers of Akan history. On the top of each linguist staff is an image known as a *finial* that references an Akan proverb. This one references the spider Ananse, who brought wisdom and weaving to the Akan people. This proverb is linked to the saying: "No one goes to the house of the spider Ananse to teach him wisdom." This could refer to the knowledge of the linguists.

Oceania

The Pacific Ocean covers about one-third of the world, and more than 25,000 islands are spread across it. Thousands of people live on these islands, which include Papua New Guinea, Hawaii, and Aotearoa. The islands are home to 2,000 different languages and cultural groups. Some cultures have been there for millennia, and some islands were populated more recently after people journeyed across the ocean in canoes. The arts of Oceania tell many stories about the people, their ancestors and history, the land, and the sea.

Kastom

People have lived in Oceania for at least 40,000 years. The word *Kastom* has been used for years by people living in New Guinea, some islands of northern Australia, Solomon Islands, and Vanuatu to describe their past and present culture, including their religious beliefs, laws, traditions, ceremonies and rituals, art, architecture, and magic.

Did you know?

In Papua New Guinea, ceremonial houses are decorated with carvings of ancestral figures. These carvings represent previous generations, but they are not meant to look like them in the way that a portrait might. Instead, the carvings represent the human form and act as a space that can contain the presence of spirits or ancestors during ceremonies. This figure, belonging to the Yimam people of the Korewori River region, has a head at the top, with a mouth, eyes, and beard. The hooks represent ribs, with a heart in the center.

Figure (*Yipwon*)
Papua New Guinea, Yimam People,
19th century or earlier

This wooden figure, which would have been kept in the men's ceremonial house, is known as a *yipwon*. It is a stylized representation of the human form. The figure's ribcage is represented as having been turned on its side, so that the ribs curve upward and downward, not sideways.

Canoe Figurehead (*Nguzu Nguzu, Musu Musu, or Toto Isu*)
Solomon Islands, possibly New Georgia Island, late 19th–early 20th century

In some islands in Oceania, people use canoes to travel and fish or to go to war, and many are lavishly adorned. As part of *Kastom*, this figurehead, known as a *nguzu nguzu, musu musu,* or *toto isu*, was attached to the front of a canoe, where it acted as a magical protector.

Feast Bowl (*Kelemui*)
Papua New Guinea, Admiralty Islands,
late 19th–early 20th century

Following *Kastom*, huge feast bowls were made for ceremonies. Carved from a single block of wood with separate handles, this would have been filled with piles of food during feasts. The coiled handles may represent the tusks, shells, or tails of animals.

Man's Comb

Solomon Islands, Ulawa Island, late 19th–early 20th century

Carefully cut and inlaid with tiny, shaped iridescent pieces of shell and coated with a black paste, this comb possibly had more decorations originally, such as feathers or tassels. A man would have worn it, usually at ceremonies and festivals, or a boy undergoing initiation rituals at puberty.

Adornment

In Solomon Islands, men wear ornate jewelry for ceremonies and to show their importance. Artists there often use carved mother-of-pearl and nautilus shell inlay, which are pieces of iridescent shells set into wooden objects that create shimmering effects. Among the adornments are combs for the hair and ornaments that embellish the ears, nose, and neck. *Kapkap* feature elaborate turtle-shell filigree (delicate, lacelike cutouts) set on top of a large, dazzling white disk of giant clam shell and look very impressive when worn on the forehead or against the chest.

Pendant or Head Ornament (*Kapkap*)

Solomon Islands, late 19th–early 20th century

Made from a range of materials found in the land and sea, this is a *kapkap*, a disk-shaped ornament created by smoothing and polishing down the large tridacna shell (giant clam) and overlaying a delicate filigree (cutout) of turtle shell. *Kapkap* are valuable items worn by men as head ornaments or as pendants around the neck.

Ear Ornament

Solomon Islands, New Georgia Island, mid-late 19th century

This ear plug would be worn in an extended hole in the earlobe. Men would pierce their ears and gradually increase the size of the hole to wear bigger and bigger plugs. You can see that the *nguzu nguzu* figure on the opposite page is wearing similar ear adornments.

Breastplate (*Tema, Tambe,* or *Tepatu*)

Solomon Islands, Santa Cruz Islands, late 19th–early 20th century

Solomon Island artists are experts at working with shells. This elaborate breastplate was made to be tied around the neck and to lay on the chest. It was created with tridacna (giant clam) shell and turtle shell. The braided fiber bindings secure the overlay to the disk and around the wearer's neck. The design of the Tema references a frigate bird and diving dolphins.

American Life

Unlike in Europe, there were no permanent academies or art museums in the United States until the 19th century. Portraiture, generally destined for private homes, was an important way patrons could display their status and identity. By mid-century, many American artists had seen some European art and studied abroad and were inspired to fashion their own hybrid styles in figure paintings that captured aspects of life at home.

Did you know?

As Paris was still seen as the art capital of the Western world in the 19th century, many artists elsewhere believed that the only way they could become successful was to study art there. So, those Americans who could afford it sailed to France to further their artistic studies. Some stayed for just a few months, others for years.

George Washington

Gilbert Stuart (American), begun 1795

This portrait of the first president of the United States was painted from life, becoming one of the most famous depictions of George Washington.

Mrs. John Winthrop

John Singleton Copley (American), 1773

Copley painted in colonial British-America and England. This portrait of Hannah Fayerweather, who was married to John Winthrop, an astronomer and a professor of mathematics and natural history at Harvard University, epitomizes the artist's pre-Revolutionary Boston style in its attention to personality and painterly textures.

William Duguid

Prince Demah Barnes (American), 1773

William Duguid moved from Scotland to Boston, where he sat for this portrait with the artist Prince Demah, who was of African descent. Demah's story is extraordinary—he is the only enslaved painter working in colonial America whose works are known to have survived.

Mr. and Mrs. I. N. Phelps Stokes

John Singer Sargent (American), 1897

This double portrait of Isaac Newton Phelps Stokes and his wife, Edith Minturn, was a wedding gift from a friend. The celebrated expatriate painter Sargent first intended to depict his subject alone and wearing an evening dress, but her dynamic arrival in his studio—and her husband's witty suggestion that he take the place of the artist's Great Dane in the background—led to this strikingly informal work.

The Chess Players

Thomas Eakins (American), 1876

Eakins, a Philadelphia-based portrait artist, painted his father observing a game of chess between two friends in a hushed, wood-paneled room, capturing the serious absorption of the players.

The Wood Sawyer

Charles E. Weir (American), 1842

This painting is unlike any known early-19th-century genre scene in its positive focus on a Black figure. The painting highlights both specific issues of urbanizing New York as well as the significant labor of a free person of color.

Ernesta (Child with Nurse)

Cecilia Beaux (American), 1894

The most celebrated woman painter in the United States in the late 19th century, Beaux produced many portraits of family and friends, including this impressionistic depiction of her two-year-old niece and favorite model, Ernesta Drinker, in motion.

American Scenes

Art in North America in the 18th and 19th centuries often celebrated the development of the nation. Artists were inspired by historical events, such as military conflicts and heroes, as well as distinctive urban and rural landscapes and populations across the continent.

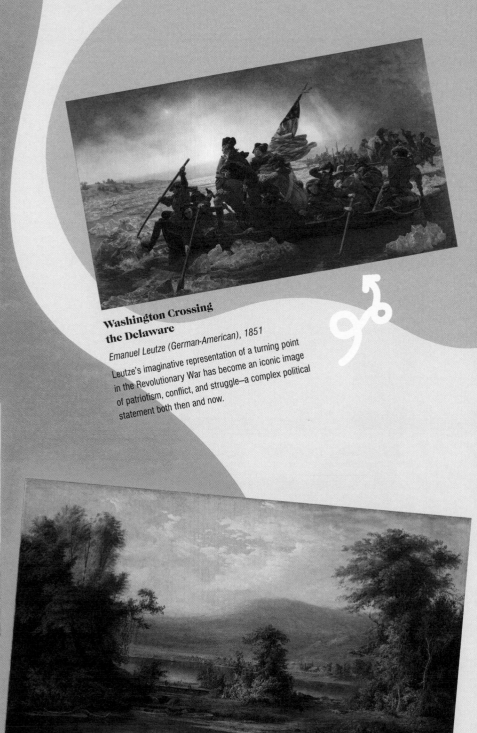

Washington Crossing the Delaware
Emanuel Leutze (German-American), 1851

Leutze's imaginative representation of a turning point in the Revolutionary War has become an iconic image of patriotism, conflict, and struggle—a complex political statement both then and now.

Fur Traders Descending the Missouri
George Caleb Bingham (American), 1845

In this tranquil and luminous scene, Bingham idealized the American frontier for the benefit of Eastern audiences while suggesting the complexity of cross-cultural family ties.

Landscape with Cows Watering in a Stream
Robert S. Duncanson (American), 1871

Born free in upstate New York, the African American painter Duncanson established an international reputation for his Hudson River School–inspired landscapes during the Civil War era. Self-taught, he began his career in Cincinnati, Ohio, where he came to the attention of abolitionist leaders, who later sponsored his study in Europe.

The Hatch Family

Eastman Johnson (American),
1870–1871

A. S. Hatch worked on Wall Street in New York City, the financial capital of North America. He was also an important collector and founder of The Metropolitan Museum of Art. Another Museum founder, Johnson depicted three generations of the wealthy family in the well-appointed library of their New York home.

Dance in a Subterranean Roundhouse at Clear Lake, California

Jules Tavernier (American), 1878

In 1876, the French-born Tavernier was commissioned to paint this haunting scene of a ceremonial dance of the Elem Pomo known as the *mfom Xe* (people dance), witnessed by the white settlers who were claiming their sacred lands for their own economic development.

A Young Mother

Bessie Potter Vonnoh (American),
1896; cast ca. 1906

Vonnoh is best known for her intimate and tender sculptures of upper-class mothers and children, popular subjects in art that appealed to broad audiences.

Girl Skating

Abastenia St. Leger Eberle (American),
1906

Roller skating was a popular pastime when Eberle depicted this child moving forward energetically on just one skate. Her statuettes of immigrant children on New York's Lower East Side focus on the joys of play rather than hardships.

Dressing for the Carnival

Winslow Homer (American), 1877

In this post–Civil War painting, Homer evokes the dislocation and endurance of African American culture that was a legacy of slavery. The central figure represents a character from a Christmas celebration known as Jonkonnu, a festival that blended African and European traditions.

Furniture

On these pages are examples of furniture from the 14th to the early 20th centuries. You can see pieces that were used to furnish holy spaces and hold religious texts (like the carved wooden stand for a Koran manuscript) as well as cabinets, desks, and even whole rooms created for royal palaces and stately homes (like the *studiolo*, or small study room, in the Ducal palace in Gubbio, Italy).

Did you know?

A mihrab, or prayer niche, is built to face the direction of Mecca—the Muslim holy pilgrimage site in Saudi Arabia—which Muslims face when praying. The example on this page from a religious school in Isfahan, Iran, is composed of a mosaic of tiny tiles. They fit together to form intricate patterns and quotations from holy texts.

Zain Hasan Sulaiman Isfahani (Iranian), Stand for a Qur'an Manuscript
Iran, dated AH 761/1360 CE

Mihrab (Prayer Niche)
Iran, dated AH 755/1354–1355 CE

Pierced Window Screen
India, second half 16th century

Cassone
Italy, ca. 1425–1450

**Armchair
(Chaise à Bras)**
*France and Italy, 15th or
16th century (textiles)
and second
half 16th century (woodwork)*

Table
French, probably 15th century

Damascus Room
Syria, dated AH 1119/1707 CE

**Johannes
Hannart
(or Jan Hanat),
Picture Frame**
*The Netherlands,
ca. 1685–1700*

**Simone Mosca,
Wall Fountain**
Italy, 1527–1534

**Francesco di Giorgio Martini,
Studiolo from the Ducal
Palace in Gubbio**
Italy, ca. 1478–1482

**Valentin Bousch,
The Prophet Isaiah**
France, 1533

**Attributed to Johann
Michael Bauer German
(Born Westheim), Settee
(One of a Pair, Part of
a Set)**
Germany, ca. 1763–1764

High Chest of Drawers
America, 1740–1760

**Stuccowork Probably by
Abbondio Stazio, Bedroom
from the Sagredo Palace**
Switzerland, ca. 1720 or later

Furniture

Sofa

J. H. Belter & Co. (American), 1850–1860

This ornate, five-legged sofa was made in the United States by the German-born American cabinetmaker John Henry Belter. To create the sofa's bold, curved form, Belter used an innovative technique of bending and compressing layers of wood with steam and pressure. Its luxurious style, inspired by 18th-century French designs, was popular with wealthy Americans in the 1850s.

Writing Table (*Bureau Plat*)

Gilles Joubert (French), 1759

This writing table—made by the French royal cabinetmaker Gilles Joubert—belonged to King Louis XV (r. 1715–1774), who kept it in his royal palace at Versailles, France. It furnished one of the most beautiful rooms of his private apartment. The desk is decorated with Asian landscape scenes in brilliant red and gold to imitate Chinese lacquer, which was very fashionable in France at the time.

Cabinet-Vitrine

*Gustave Serrurier-Bovy (Belgian),
1899*

Writing Table

*Jean-François Oeben (French),
ca. 1721–1763*

Pair of Doors

*Lorenzo de Ferrari (Italian),
ca. 1743–1744*

Library Table

*Herter Brothers
(American), 1879–1882*

Side Table

*Edward William Godwin (British),
ca. 1872*

Cabinet

*Émile-Jacques Ruhlmann
(French), ca. 1918–1919*

Revolving Chair

*United Society of Believers
in Christ's Second Appearing
(American, Shaker), 1840–1870*

Rolltop Desk

*David Roentgen
(German),
ca. 1776–1779*

Coin Cabinet

*Probably
François-Honoré-
Georges
Jacob-Desmalter
(French), ca. 1805*

Fashion

The fine clothes pictured on these pages were all once the height of fashion—from the wide skirts of the Robe à l'Anglaise (number 13) to the slender silk gown designed by designer Mariano Fortuny in the 1930s (number 6). Crafted in luxurious fabrics like silk or velvet, embroidered with gold thread, and finished with ribbon and lace, these outfits offer a glimpse of the many ways in which fashion has changed over the centuries.

1

2

1. Dress (American), 1832–1835 **2.** Evening Dress, Gabrielle Chanel (French), 1939 **3.** Dinner Dress, Lucien Lelong (French), spring/summer 1940, and Dinner Dress, Madame Grès (French), ca. 1939 **4.** "The Rice Bowl Dress," Carolyn Schnurer (American), 1952 **5.** "Velázquez" Dress, Cristobal Balenciaga (Spanish), 1939 **6.** Dress, Mariano Fortuny (Spanish), Fortuny (Italian), 1920–1940 **7.** Riding Jacket (British), ca. 1760 **8.** Dress, Christian Dior (French), 1947 **9.** Men's Wedding Shirt (Spanish), 18th century **10.** Coat (French), ca. 1750 **11** Child's Dress (American), mid-18th century **12.** Evening Dress, Jeanne Paquin (French), winter 1905 **13.** Robe à l'Anglaise (British), 1740–1760 **14.** Doublet (French), early 1620s **15.** Tea Gown, Cristobal Balenciaga (Spanish), 1937 **16.** Evening Dress, Elsa Schiaparelli (Italian), ca. 1939 **17.** Dress (American), 1860–1865 **18.** Cape (Spanish), 17th century **19.** Jerkin (British), 1610–1625 **20.** "Clover Leaf" Dress, Charles James (American), 1953 **21.** Jacket (British), ca. 1616 **22.** Robe à la Française (French), 1770–1775 **23.** Evening Dress, Madeleine Vionnet (French), ca. 1936 **24.** Evening Apron, Attributed to Mainbocher (American), 1930–1939 **25.** Ensemble (Russian), third quarter 17th–19th century **26.** Waistcoat (French), 1760-1770

Undergarments and Accessories

Accessories like the ones here completed stylish outfits—for example, the Russian hats and the French parasol. Undergarments like the British panniers helped shape full, flowing skirts—so wide that the wearer had to go through doors sideways!

Shoes
British, 1790–1825

Parasol, Dupuy
French, 1900–1908

Hat
Russian, fourth quarter 18th century

Hat

Caroline Reboux (French),
1911–1913

Bustle

British, ca. 1871

Panniers

British, ca. 1750

Adornment

Choosing a necklace, bracelet, or other ornament to wear can be an important expression of identity. It might signal respect for a religious ceremony, show love for a traditional craft, or add a sense of luxury or status.

01

Brooch in the Form of an Owl Head

Firm of Castellani, ca. 1860

02

Peacock Feather Brooch

Europe, last quarter 19th century

03

Headdress Ornament

Iran, 19th century

06

Earring

Eastern Tibet, 19th century

04

Bracelet: Four Figures

Edo Peoples, 19th century

05

Bracelet with Makara Head Terminals

India, 19th century

07

Ankle Bells

Dan Peoples, Wobe, early 19th century

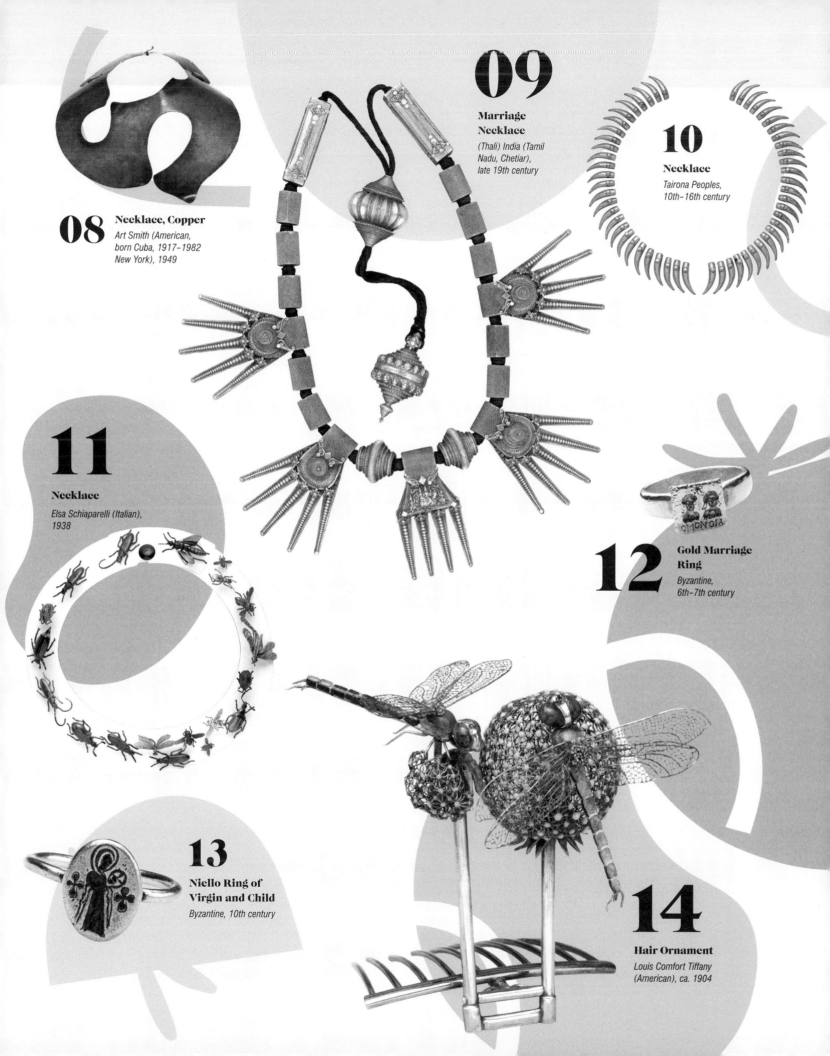

08 **Necklace, Copper**

Art Smith (American, born Cuba, 1917–1982 New York), 1949

09

Marriage Necklace

(Thali) India (Tamil Nadu, Chetiar), late 19th century

10

Necklace

Tairona Peoples, 10th–16th century

11

Necklace

Elsa Schiaparelli (Italian), 1938

12 **Gold Marriage Ring**

Byzantine, 6th–7th century

13

Niello Ring of Virgin and Child

Byzantine, 10th century

14 **Hair Ornament**

Louis Comfort Tiffany (American), ca. 1904

4.

THE MODERN AGE

Nature

In the late 1800s, a new generation of European artists was challenging the way art was taught, created, and viewed. To them, it felt confining to paint grand canvases about history and mythology in the studio. They started a revolution in art by painting outside and letting the light and colors of nature be their guide. Painters discovered that even a simple scene, like a haystack in a field, could appear totally different as the time of day or the season changed. Meanwhile, photographers pioneered new techniques to capture the ever-changing light and movement of the natural world.

Still Life with a Ginger Jar and Eggplants

Paul Cézanne (French), 1893–1894

Unlike the Impressionists, Cézanne painted fruit that had been taken out of nature and brought inside, in scenes called "still lifes." He made the everyday objects he painted dynamic. This plate of pears seems ready to slide away. The jars have impossible angles, as if we are looking at them from multiple perspectives, and the fabric takes on a life of its own.

The Rocky Mountains, Lander's Peak

Albert Bierstadt (American), 1863

Stunning landscapes like this, based on scenery Bierstadt saw on expeditions, helped shape how Americans saw the West. But such romantic visions had a huge cost for Native Americans. Peoples like the Shoshone pictured here lost traditional lands, ways of life, and resources as the United States expanded.

Impressionists painted outside so they could observe nature.

Impressionism

In 1872, Claude Monet painted *Impression, Sunrise*. Many people who first saw it thought it was unfinished. One critic used the painting's title to make fun of Monet and his peers, calling them "Impressionists." The name stuck, but the artists took it as a compliment! Their goal wasn't to represent nature clearly but to capture how we experience a scene in the moment.

Morning on the Seine near Giverny

Claude Monet (French), 1897

Spiraea Aruncus (Tyrol)
Anna Atkins (British), 1851–1854

Atkins followed state-of-the-art developments in photography during her time. This cyanotype photogram was made by placing plant samples directly onto paper and letting the sun develop the image. This work is the earliest photograph by a woman in The Met's collection.

The Ascent of Mont Blanc
Auguste-Rosalie Bisson (French), 1861

Bisson needed dozens of helpers carrying heavy loads of equipment to take this photo on the highest peak of the Alps. While it is staged to look like the group are climbing up, Bisson actually took the shot when the group was coming down.

Photographing Nature

The practice of photography developed over years of artistic and scientific experiments. In the early 19th century, inventors began figuring out how to use light-sensitive chemicals. The first problem was how to capture details, instead of just shadows. The next problem was how to "fix" an image with chemicals, so it didn't disappear after printing. Then, photographers needed to turn negative images into positive images. Thanks to advances by Henry Fox Talbot, Louis Daguerre, and others, photography began to take off worldwide in the 1840s. By the mid-19th century, some artists were using the medium to respond to nature. Camera in hand, they tackled subjects outdoors, from botany to mountain climbing.

Winter Trees, Reflected in a Pond
William Henry Fox Talbot (British), 1842–1843

Some artists used photography to capture what they saw in nature. Look at how William Henry Fox Talbot has captured the reflection of trees on the surface of the pond in this artwork.

Cities

Cities got extreme makeovers in the 19th century. Paris was a labyrinth of cramped and crooked streets before Baron Georges-Eugène Haussmann cleared space for wide avenues and parks. Not everyone was happy, calling him "the demolisher"! London changed dramatically too. Joseph Bazalgette engineered an impressive sewer system and embankments along the Thames River. Marc Brunel and his son Isambard did what some thought impossible, creating a tunnel underneath the river. In Europe and the United States, more and more people moved from the countryside to the city. They moved from farming and small-scale trades to working in large factories. Sometimes, city life offered new independence and opportunities. But it could also be dangerous. Artists depicted the many changes that came with industrialization and showed the inequality in how it affected people.

The Boulevard Montmartre on a Winter Morning
Camille Pissarro (French), 1897
Pissarro was one of the earliest and most important modern Jewish artists. He had a special gift for capturing light in different weather and seasons, as in this scene depicting Monmartre, an area of Paris that was popular with many famous artists.

Vehicles on the Streets of Tokyo

Utagawa Yoshitora (Japanese),1870

Life in Tokyo changed rapidly in the late 19th century. Yoshitora shows a city on the move, full of change and new technology.

Printmaking

The 19th century saw many advances in printmaking. In Japan, artists like Hokusai and Yoshitora made brilliant multicolored woodblock prints of everything from snowcapped Mount Fuji to street life in Edo (Tokyo). These prints became a major source of inspiration for modern artists in Europe. Van Gogh bought lots of these prints, and he even wrote to his brother: "All my work is based to some extent on Japanese art..."

Mechanization

In the 19th century, factories developed new machines to increase efficiency, promising easier labor and cheaper products. But the reality was more complicated. Factory life could be dangerous and poorly paid, and traditional crafts and ways of life started to disappear. Some groups, like the Luddites in England, intentionally broke machines, believing that they were ruining people's quality of life.

Moulin Rouge: La Goulue
Henri de Toulouse-Lautrec (French), 1891

Toulouse-Lautrec was a frequent visitor to the Moulin Rouge
(Red Windmill) club in Paris. Growing up, he had been bullied for
his looks, especially his short legs. At the Moulin Rouge, with all its
different characters, Toulouse-Lautrec felt accepted and at home.
He even created this printed poster, an advertisement for the club
that became world-famous.

Leisure

Today, we might take weekends for granted, but the idea of
not working all week is the result of hard-won campaigns for
workers' rights in 19th-century Europe and the United States.
For the first time, people of all classes were free to enjoy a full
afternoon relaxing. London, New York, and especially Paris
also became famous for their nightlife. Paris boasted cabarets
offering comedy, music, and acrobatic dances like the
can-can that captured the imagination of artists, including
Toulouse-Lautrec.

Post-Impressionism

Impressionism shook up the academic tradition of
painting, but it was only the beginning. In the years
that followed, artists challenged every convention.
Instead of trying to paint representationally, they
challenged viewers to see in new ways. Artists like
Toulouse-Lautrec explored flat, sometimes unusual
colors not connected to nature, challenging the
expectation that a canvas represented a real space.

Circus Sideshow (*Parade de cirque*)
Georges Seurat (French), 1887–1888

Sideshows were free shows held outside a circus tent. They
were meant to tempt people to buy tickets and come inside.
Seurat used his signature style of pointillism, combining
thousands of tiny dots of different colors, to create this gaslit
nighttime scene.

The Rehearsal of the Ballet Onstage
Edgar Degas (French), ca. 1874

Performance

Ballet, opera, and theater thrived in Paris. While the performances were impressive, artists like Cassatt and Degas were just as interested in what happened offstage. They painted performers practicing behind the curtains as well as wealthy audiences up in the balconies, socializing in their finest outfits. The most enviable place to see and be seen was the Palais Garnier, which opened in 1875 and became the largest opera house in the world.

**The Champion Single Sculls
(Max Schmitt in a Single Scull)**

Thomas Eakins (American), 1871

In this artwork depicting men taking part in the sport of sculling, Eakins has painted himself rowing the middle boat. He was an avid rower himself.

The Bouquet of Violets

Eva Gonzalès (French), ca. 1877–1878

Gonzalès's sister Jeanne was probably the model for this painting, depicting a woman about to place a bouquet of violets in a vase.

Lydia Crocheting in the Garden at Marly

Mary Cassatt (American), 1880

While male artists got more attention, female Impressionists like Cassatt, Morisot, and Gonzalès played an important role in the movement. Today, their works are celebrated both for their technique and their depiction of women's daily lives, especially in and around the home. The subject here is Cassatt's sister.

Self-Portraits

In earlier centuries, portraits primarily focused on royalty and nobility. In the modern period, artists have enjoyed more flexibility and freedom to explore depicting other subjects, including themselves. Self-portraits provided a unique opportunity to look inward and explore psychology as this new field developed in the 20th century.

1. Self-Portrait, Käthe Kollwitz (German), no date **2.** Untitled Self-Portrait, Mose Tolliver (American), 1987 **3.** Blue Deb, Deborah Kass (American), 2012 **4.** Self-Portrait, Andy Warhol (American), 1986 **5.** Self Portrait, II, Horace Pippin (American), 1944 **6.** Three Studies for Self-Portrait, Francis Bacon (British), 1979–1980 **7.** Self-Portrait with Open Mouth, Avigdor Arikha (Israeli, born Romania), 1973 **8.** Self-Portrait, Lee Krasner (American), ca. 1929 **9.** Photomatic Enunciation Piece ("Anything Goes"), Vito Acconci (American), 1969 **10.** Self-Portrait, Pablo Picasso, 1906 **11.** Self-Portrait, Francesco Clemente (Italian), 2005

5

6

9

7

8

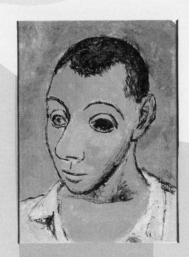

10

11

Form

Artists in the early 20th century began to take new risks with form. Some developed complex new styles like Cubism, which represented different views of a subject at the same time. Others focused on simplicity, eliminating any element that wasn't needed to express the essence of their subject. Many found inspiration in the art of different cultures, from the wooden masks of West Africa to the massive stone sculptures of Central America.

Brancusi

Brancusi grew up in the mountains of Romania, where he learned to carve wooden tools and eventually sculptures. When he moved to Paris, he met like-minded artists working with new forms. He was interested in exploring the essence or idea behind his subjects. There is no defined head or beak in Brancusi's Bird in Space, here on the right. The artwork focuses more on what it feels like for a bird to soar through the sky than its physical form.

Bird in Space

Constantin Brancusi (French, born Romania), 1923

A version of this sculpture was the subject of a court case in the United States. Officials said it wasn't art and should be taxed like "Kitchen Utensils and Hospital Supplies"!

Jeanne Hébuterne

Amedeo Modigliani (Italian), 1919

Modigliani painted his partner Jeanne Hébuterne many times. In this painting, he extends her arms and the finger resting on her cheek in unexpected ways. The features flow together perfectly, giving the picture a graceful elegance of balanced forms.

Woman in a Chemise in an Armchair

Pablo Picasso (Spanish), late 1913–early 1914

This work is an important example of synthetic Cubism. In this period, Picasso began to combine many different sources. As he often did, here he took inspiration from West African sculptures and masks.

Cubism

Pablo Picasso and his friend Georges Braque invented a style called Cubism in 1907–1908. In the first years of Cubism, artists analyzed subjects and presented them as many different facets, or planes, all at once. Some artists introduced newspaper clippings or sheet music into their paintings.

Color

Picasso and the Cubists changed how people thought about form. Other modern artists wanted to do the same for color. Matisse and his friends became known as Fauves, or wild beasts, because of their unconventional color choices that often departed from nature. Other painters, including the Expressionists, used unexpected color combinations to explore the unsettling aspects of modern life.

Duncan Grant in Front of a Mirror

Vanessa Stephen Bell (British), ca. 1915–1917

Bell was a leading member of the Bloomsbury Group in England, along with her sister, author Virginia Woolf. This painting is of Bell's companion, artist Duncan Grant. Its bright colors show the interest in color as a way to express feeling.

Improvisation 27 (Garden of Love II)

Vasily Kandinsky (French, born Russia), 1912

The Russian artist Wassily Kandinsky gave musical titles to many of his paintings, including words such as *improvisation*, like the title of this work. He thought that colors trigger different senses. To Kandinsky, yellow—like the center of this painting—was exciting and sounded like a trumpet. He believed that blue, seen here in the corner, created a calm and soothing sensation. The scene may be inspired by the story of the Garden of Eden.

The Cathedrals of Broadway
Florine Stettheimer (American), 1929
Here, Stettheimer depicts Broadway's theaters, their names in lights. She celebrated the spectacle of New York City's theater district in vibrant color and animated form.

Let My People Go
Aaron Douglas (American), ca. 1935-1939
Douglas was part of the Harlem Renaissance, a movement of Black creatives based in New York. The title of this painting reflects Moses's words to the pharaoh—a powerful story for African Americans seeking freedom and equality. A bright yellow light splits the composition, illuminating Moses and revealing God's favor. In the purple shadows, pharaoh's soldiers on horseback are swallowed by the Red Sea as they pursue the escaping Israelites.

Tables for Ladies
Edward Hopper (American), 1930
Hopper often painted scenes of city life. He excelled at capturing the mood of places like offices or restaurants at night, which could feel isolating. Hopper's carefully chosen colors—especially his use of yellow—emphasizes the artificial light of the restaurant.

The Blue Period

Picasso became one of the most famous and successful artists of the 20th century. But as a young man, his life was very different. After his best friend died, Picasso went through a period of depression, painting lonely figures in moody colors in what became known as his Blue Period. When he recovered, Picasso reversed his palette and started creating happier scenes featuring women, children, and circus performers. That became his Rose Period.

The Blind Man's Meal
Pablo Picasso (Spanish), 1903

Time

The world was changing fast in the early 20th century, with cars and airplanes revolutionizing travel. Some saw danger and chaos in this speed, especially after the turmoil of World War I. Others, like the artists known as the Futurists, found the speed of modern life thrilling. The Dada movement used nonsense to criticize people who put too much faith in power, technology, and politics. Other artists responded to this period by creating art that felt timeless and dreamy.

Ariadne
Giorgio de Chirico (Italian, born Greece), 1913

The sculpture in this painting suggests classical Greece, but the steam train is modern. It makes the viewer feel lost, as the title hints. In Greek mythology, Ariadne gave Theseus a thread to save him from getting lost in a labyrinth.

Unique Forms of Continuity in Space
Umberto Boccioni (Italian), 1913, cast 1950

In Italy, Boccioni was one of the leaders of the Futurist movement, alongside peers like Tommaso Marinetti and Gino Severini. These painters, poets, and theorists were interested in finding fresh forms for a new era and sweeping away old traditions and institutions. Boccioni's sculpture ripples with energy and feels like it is rushing into the future.

Weltrevolution (World Revolution)
Hannah Höch (German), 1920

Höch was skilled at photomontage—pasting together clippings from photos and newspapers. She used it to reflect the confusion of the period between the two World Wars, especially in Germany. The word *Dada*, referring to the Dada movement, is included in the image.

The Dada Movement

The Dada movement was born out of the hopelessness of World War I. The optimism of movements like Futurism felt inappropriate to many in the wake of such destruction and loss of life. Dadaist poets, musicians, and artists did not produce a single style. They used many different forms of expression—including nonsensical ideas and words—to critique authority figures and traditional ideas. Rather than projecting a glorious future, they were concerned with expressing the strange reality of the present.

America Today (Detail)
Thomas Hart Benton (American), 1930–1931

This panel is one part of a room-sized mural. It depicts work and pastimes in places the artist visited around the United States. Even in the midst of the Depression, Benton showed the United States in this panel of the mural racing toward the future and making advances in technology.

Painting Memories

Some artists explored the theme of time by drawing on their memories of the past. Marc Chagall grew up in Russia. After more than 50 years in France, he continued to return to themes of his Jewish childhood in the small town of Vitebsk. Chagall's paintings mix real memories with imagination. Looking at one feels like stepping into a fairy tale, where people and animals fly through the air, and everything looks topsy-turvy.

Lovers Among Lilacs
Marc Chagall (French), 1930

The Repast of the Lion
Henri Rousseau (Le Douanier) (French), ca. 1907

Even though Rousseau never saw the jungle in person, he re-created it again and again in his paintings, sometimes inspired by botanical gardens in Paris. His scenes of wild animals often feel like timeless dreamscapes, as primal and mysterious today as they were when he painted them. While he was largely self-trained, Rousseau earned the admiration of Picasso and others of his circle.

Bold Abstractions

In abstract art, color and form aren't just tools for expressing a subject—they *are* the subject! Even if it looks simple, abstract art often still involves a lot of careful planning.

1

1. Composition, Piet Mondrian (Dutch), 1921 2. Pintura Constructiva, Joaquín Torres-García (Uruguayan), 1931 3. Alakzat IV (Formation IV), Imre Bak (Hungarian), 1969 4. Homage to the Square: On Near Sky, Josef Albers (American, born Germany), 1963 5. Mecca, Hans Hofmann (American, born Germany), 1961 6. No. 13 (White, Red on Yellow), Mark Rothko (American, born Russia), 1958 7. Inner Edge, Helen Frankenthaler (American), 1966 8. May Picture, Paul Klee (German, born Switzerland), 1925 9. Second Theme, Burgoyne Diller (American), 1938–1940

Surrealism

Artists often rely on imagination. But the Surrealists took this to new levels, finding subject matter in places like dreams and desires. Some Surrealists, like Joan Miró, created abstract forms in their work, which seem to have a life of their own. Other Surrealists painted everyday objects in surprising situations, like the stones in Salvador Dalí's painting here.

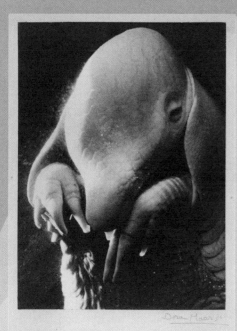

Père Ubu

Dora Maar (French), 1936

Maar created many surrealist photographs. This one refers to the character in a play, but the photo is a real animal: a baby armadillo.

Self-Portrait

Leonora Carrington (Mexican, born England), ca. 1937–1938

Carrington was frustrated with the social constraints of English life. She moved to France, where she engaged with many Surrealists. She insisted on her own creative voice, saying, "I didn't have time to be anyone's muse... I was too busy rebelling against my family and learning to be an artist." During World War II, she fled France for Mexico, where she found fresh inspiration in traditional myths, folklore, and art, especially involving animals.

Tapping the Unconscious

The Surrealists were inspired by major developments in the field of psychology in the early 20th century. The Austrian doctor Sigmund Freud was especially influential. Freud studied dreams and asked patients to do "free association" of ideas to help him understand their thoughts, especially the desires he believed were repressed. For Surrealists, repressed desires were a creative goldmine! Surrealists were also inspired by Freud's notion of the uncanny, in which objects that otherwise might feel familiar are unfamiliar and feel unsettling.

The Barbarians

Max Ernst (French, born Germany), 1937

Ernst painted many images of strange, imaginary creatures in equally mysterious landscapes. This imagery was especially powerful at a time of great uncertainty, on the brink of World War II. The artist narrowly escaped from France to the United States during the war.

The Accommodations of Desire
Salvador Dalí (Spanish), 1929

Dalí takes what seem to be simple objects—pebbles lying on a beach—and makes them strange and fantastical. Here, he combines a highly detailed painterly style with collage, cutting out an image of a lion from a children's book and placing the head, mouth, and mane on different rocks.

Potato
Joan Miró (Spanish), 1928

In the 1920s, Miró produced several paintings inspired by his family's farm in Catalonia, a region in Spain with a strong sense of its own tradition and culture. Miró dug into his Catalan heritage throughout his career. Here, he paints a female figure above a field, initially made from unconscious doodle forms, with a potato floating curiously in front of her face.

Draw like a Surrealist

Fold a piece of paper into sections, accordion-style, so you can only see one section at a time. Make a drawing of an animal or human head on the top section. Now, fold that over and pass the paper to a friend. Have them draw the body of a creature, real or imagined. Now, have that person fold it over again and draw some legs. Unfold the piece of paper and see what being you've created. This was a game the Surrealists did themselves, called *cadavre exquis*, or exquisite corpse.

Cadavre Exquis (Exquisite Corpse)
André Breton (French), Valentine Hugo (French), 1932

Perfume Bottle
Elsa Schiaparelli (Italian), Leonor Fini (Italian, born Argentina), ca. 1937

Schiaparelli came from a wealthy, traditional family. She rebelled and was determined to make her own creative path. She founded a fashion house and collaborated with some of the most famous Surrealists of her time. With Salvador Dalí, she created a makeup case that looked like the top of a phone dial and a dress with a lobster design. She created a line of signature perfumes with unique bottles. This one is based on a dressmaker's dummy, which even has a tiny measuring tape on it.

Finding Form

Europe produced a parade of modern art movements from the late 19th century onward. By the mid-20th century, the balance of power in the art world was shifting. Innovative groups were springing up across the globe. New York City was one such hub for experimentation, attracting artists from diverse backgrounds, hungry for opportunities and recognition. Artists made bold statements by exploring abstraction, making art that didn't necessarily represent the world visually but spoke its own language of shapes and colors.

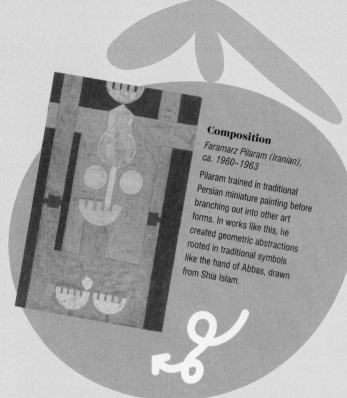

Composition

Faramarz Pilaram (Iranian), ca. 1960–1963

Pilaram trained in traditional Persian miniature painting before branching out into other art forms. In works like this, he created geometric abstractions rooted in traditional symbols like the hand of Abbas, drawn from Shia Islam.

Concord

Barnett Newman (American), 1949

Art does not have to be complicated to be powerful. Newman realized that the simple act of painting a line could define the space of a painting and captivate the viewer. For more than 20 years, he experimented with endless variations on this idea, using vertical lines he called "zips."

Carousel State

Sam Gilliam (American), 1968

Gilliam broke down the distinction between painting and sculpture. His famous "drape paintings" are pinned up without any frame, allowing them to create a rhythm in three dimensions instead of two.

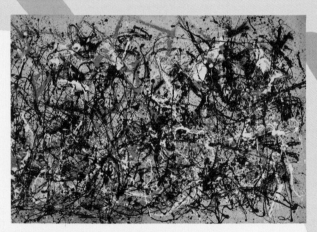

Autumn Rhythm (Number 30)

Jackson Pollock (American), 1950

Pollock turned the practice of painting upside down. First, he painted the canvas on the floor. This meant that he could paint even bigger and walk around his work from every angle. Next, instead of brushing paint onto the canvas, he would fling and flick it from a distance, letting it spatter in beautiful patterns.

Women Making Waves

Women were key players in every aspect of the American art scene. Betty Parsons and Peggy Guggenheim ran influential galleries in New York City. Louise Nevelson was a leading sculptor, as well as a style icon with a flair for the dramatic. Helen Frankenthaler used a new technique, pouring and soaking paint into her canvases. Alma Thomas and Carmen Herrera are recognized as major pioneers for their bright hues and geometric forms.

Oval Form with Strings and Color
Barbara Hepworth (British), 1966

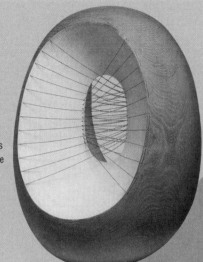

Hepworth took a novel approach to sculpture. Instead of working inside-out, she worked outside-in, exploring the spaces within forms. Her sculptures frequently have holes and gaps, sometimes with delicate strings stretched across them, like instruments from another world.

Take Off
Helen Frankenthaler (American), 1956

Frankenthaler explored many ways of applying paint. Sometimes, she would drip and pour paint onto the canvas. Other times, she used brushes to create forms and then partly cover them up, as she did here. She often allowed accident to play a role in her works—one of her paintings even shows the paw print of a cat that walked across the surface!

Iberic
Carmen Herrera (Cuban-American), 1949

Although the Cuban-American artist was friends with major contemporary abstract artists like Barnett Newman, Herrera received little recognition and few exhibition opportunities until she was nearly 90! Her hard-edged abstractions feature strong contrasts that push and pull the viewer's gaze in bold, experimental ways.

Red Roses Sonata
Alma Thomas (American), 1972

Thomas was one of the most important Black women artists of her time. Her signature style uses short brushstrokes that follow one another in sophisticated patterns, evoking musical rhythms. These intricate strokes fit together into large, striking shapes like concentric circles or shimmering rows, as in this work.

Everyday Life

Abstraction was more popular than ever at mid-century. But there were still plenty of artists who wanted to make art that reflected the world around them, recalling the way Cubists had used everyday objects. For some mid-century artists, like Pop artists, this meant creating works inspired by all the things they saw in movies, comics, billboards, and magazines. For others, it meant shining a light on poverty and injustice through documentary photographs or public art. By the 1970s, the boundary between art and everyday life was getting harder and harder to see, let alone maintain.

Tomato from Campbell's Soup I

Andy Warhol (American), 1968

The best Pop artists, like Andy Warhol, make us think about what we buy and how images influence us. Warhol created pictures of everything from cans of soup and Coca-Cola to celebrities like Marilyn Monroe and Elvis Presley.

The Block

Romare Bearden (American), 1971

This collage is 18 ft (5.5 m) long, giving viewers the experience of walking along a city block in New York. It captures the vibrant rhythms of Black life in Harlem, including a church, barbershop, apartments, and storefronts. Originally, the work was even exhibited with recordings of street noise playing in the background. Bearden was a cultural leader in Harlem and also an important author who drew attention to other Black artists.

Mrs. N's Palace

Louise Nevelson (American, born Ukraine), 1964–1977

Nevelson began her sculptures by collecting discarded wood, including everything from chairs to toilet seats. She always worked in one color at a time, usually black. Looking at this sculpture, you can see why Nevelson called herself "The Architect of Shadow."

Filipinos Cutting Lettuce, Salinas, California

Dorothea Lange (American), 1935

Lange took some of the most famous photos of the Great Depression, a period of biting poverty in the United States. She had deep sympathy for people forced to work on farms in terrible conditions for almost no money. She felt it was important for an artist not to be "taking anything away from anyone: their privacy, their dignity, their wholeness." By photographing these workers at ground level, looking up, she gives them the monumental scale and power of classical sculptures.

Winter Pool

Robert Rauschenberg (American), 1959

Rauschenberg was restless and inventive. This is an example of what he called his "combines." These mixed painting with everyday objects, like clothing, photographs, and even a ladder. Viewers can imagine climbing up the ladder and leaping into the work itself or, indeed, the cold and empty "winter pool" suggested by the title.

Chairs

A chair is a space for a person to sit. That might seem simple enough, but this purpose can take on almost infinite forms. Sitting can be a formal ritual, an expression of community, part of conversing or eating, or an opportunity for relaxation. Some artists and artisans have created designs that reconfigure how we sit and even how we think about sitting.

01

Tête-à-Tête
*Attributed to
John Henry Belter
(German), 1850–1860*

02

Side Chair
*Herter Brothers
(American), 1879–1882*

03 **"Butterfly" Stool**
*Sori Yanagi (Japanese), designed
1954; manufactured 1987*

04

Folding chair
*Northern African or Syrian for the
European market, second half
19th century*

05

A Garden Chair
Georges Braque (French), 1947–1960

06
Victorian Interior II
Horace Pippin (American),
1945

07
Zig Zag Stoel
*Designer Gerrit Rietveld
(Dutch), ca. 1937–1940*

08
Chair
*Guere Peoples, possibly
20th century*

09
Elks Club
*William Wegman
(American), 1980*

10
Rietveld Chair
*Sarah Charlesworth
(American), 1981*

12
Iya Ati Omo
Yinka Ilori (British-Nigerian), 2016

11
London Papardelle
Ron Arad (British), 1992

New Experiments

In the second half of the 20th century, artists experimented with new kinds of art making, including performance. One of their goals was to test the limits of what is considered art. For some, that meant emphasizing the thought process behind the work rather than the finished product. Another goal was to make art less commercial, focusing on a unique experience that couldn't be duplicated, bought, or sold.

Lette Eisenhauer Ascending Ladder in "The Courtyard," a Happening by Allan Kaprow (American), New York City
Lawrence N. Shustak (American), 1962

Semiotics of the Kitchen
Martha Rosler (American), 1975

This is a still from a video of a piece of performance art by Martha Rosler. Rosler criticized prejudiced expectations about women's place in society, especially in the home. With deadpan humor, she parodied cookery demonstrations by picking up instruments from knives to nutcrackers in alphabetical order, and acting out their use.

Bandit 201
Robert Watts (American), 1967

Art as Actions

Performance art is a fluid form, which can involve brief informal activities or stretch into complicated actions. Allan Kaprow called his performances "happenings." The photograph on the left of this page captures one such happening, where viewers and passersby watched as a woman used a ladder to ascend a mysterious mountain. Other artists invited people to participate in art themselves through small acts, like Robert Watts, who created stick-on tattoos (here on the left). By wearing these tattoos, people took part in the work of art.

III

Lorna Simpson (American), 1994

Simpson examines issues of identity, often
connected to her experience as a Black woman.
Here, she creates wishbones in clay, rubber,
and bronze. By making wishbones that might
break, bend, or remain firm, she invites viewers
to think about what we believe is possible.

**Wrapped Building,
Project for 1 Times
Square, Allied
Chemical Tower,
New York**

*Christo (American, born
Bulgaria), Jeanne-Claude
(American), 1991*

Wrapped Newspaper

*Christo (American, born Bulgaria),
Jeanne-Claude (American), 1980–1981*

Wrapping Objects

The husband-and-wife team
Christo and Jeanne-Claude
were known for wrapping
objects, like the newspaper
pictured here. They also
wrapped entire buildings;
pictured on the left is a
proposal for an idea to wrap
a New York skyscraper.
By covering things up, Christo
and Jeanne-Claude turned
them into a mystery waiting
to be revealed, like a present.

Art and Activism

Many modern movements in the early 1900s glorified life in the city. By the late 20th century, artists still flocked to cities, determined to show the gritty, difficult parts of urban life. By sharing their experiences with brutal honesty, artists of color and LGBTQ+ artists helped change misperceptions and prejudice, both within the art world and beyond.

Speaking Out Through Art

One of the most urgent issues in the 1980s and '90s was the HIV-AIDS epidemic. Many governments did little for treatment or research and sometimes barely even acknowledged the disease. Artists, especially members of the LGBTQ+ community, took matters into their own hands, making art that confronted their pain and society's silence.

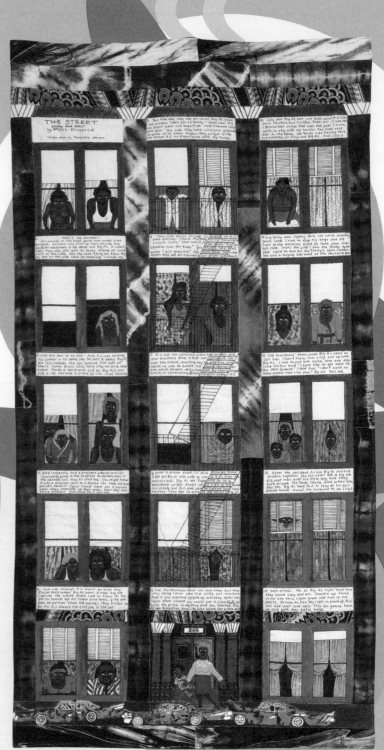

Attorney Street (Handball Court with Autobiographical Poem by Piñero)

Martin Wong (American), 1982–1984

Wong was Chinese-American and grew up in San Francisco before moving to New York City. There, his friend, poet Miguel Piñero, introduced him to the "Nuyorican" cultural scene led by Puerto Ricans. Even though he was not deaf, Wong often used fingerspelling from American Sign Language in his work, reflecting on the city as a place of multiple languages, in which minority groups often depend on the power and protection of gestures and codes.

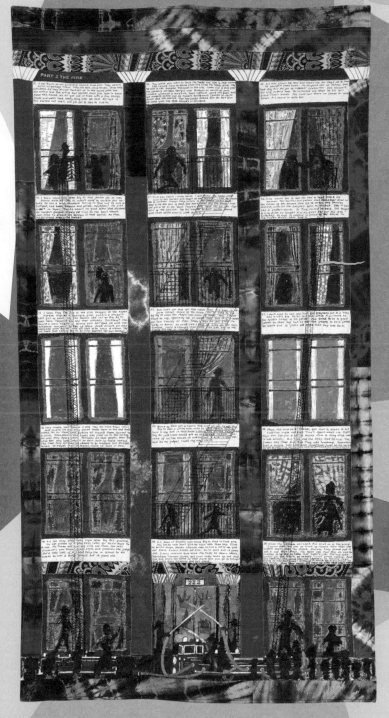

Street Story Quilt

Faith Ringgold (American), 1985

Ringgold combines many media, from painting to textile art. She is also an activist and addresses the inequalities experienced by African Americans. Ringgold is a famous children's book artist, too, and her book *Tar Beach* includes imagery from her quilts. Her use of quilts proudly connects her work to female African American artists of past generations, who designed quilts with inventive patterns that referenced their lives and struggles.

History and Memory

The 20th century saw incredible achievements as well as conflict and exploitation. Artists at the end of the century played a key role in exploring this complicated history. Above all, they have helped amplify the voices and memories of people whose experiences were often ignored by earlier generations. Art can change not only history but also how history is written and studied.

Did you know?

The word *diaspora* comes from the Greek word for "scattering" or "dispersion." It originally referred to ancient Israelites forced out of their homeland and to the Jewish communities that formed around the world in later centuries. Now, the word can refer to any community living outside their traditional place of origin. In art history, the term *diaspora* is used to contextualize the experiences of artists who have relocated to other parts of the world, new communities formed in such places, and works of art that depict these experiences.

Heavy Cloud
Anselm Kiefer (German), 1985

Kiefer's artworks are often heavy, both physically and metaphorically. Here, he replaces clouds in a landscape photograph with lead. The work might refer to nuclear power and bombs. But the lead could also symbolize the weight of history itself—Kiefer was born in 1945, right at the end of World War II. Throughout his career, Kiefer has often used themes and iconography from Jewish texts and traditions to inspire his work. This image can also be read as a reference to the Israelites' Exodus from Egypt, in which it was believed that "The Lord went in front of them in a pillar of cloud by day" to lead the way through the desert (Exodus 13:21, NRSV).

Four Hundred Years of Free Labor
Joe Minter (American), 1995

This sculpture symbolizes the toil of enslaved African Americans and their exploitation even after Emancipation. Minter is an outsider artist, who has spent more than 30 years making a massive installation in Alabama that he calls The African Village in America.

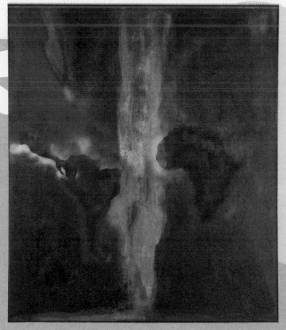

Night Journey

Frank Bowling (British), 1969–1970

Bowling was born in Guyana and moved to London to study art. His work often mixes abstraction and figuration. Here, he uses bright yellow to highlight the Middle Passage between Africa and the Americas, where millions of enslaved people lost their lives and freedom in the colonial period.

Migration

The 20th century involved enormous migration. Sometimes, people moved because they wanted new experiences or opportunities. Many times, people moved because they had to, under threat. Artists reflected this movement and people's stories in their work.

The Wine Dark Sea

Hew Locke (British), 2016

Locke is the British-Guyanese son of two artists. His boat sculptures hang from the ceiling, so viewers wade through them. They are made to look ramshackle, like boats used by people in desperate circumstances, especially refugees and migrants.

The Refusal of Time

William Kentridge (South African), 2012

While Kentridge does not view himself as an activist, his works often explore the problems of how to memorialize and process the pain and shame of South Africa's history of Apartheid. He has used elements from theater, puppetry, and animation in his drawings, films, and installations, which reflect on how we stage and perform memory. Here, he references systems and machines from the history of science to explore how we "tell" time.

Digital Art

Artists have always experimented with new technology to make art, including the pottery wheel and the printing press. In the 21st century, artists have an abundance of new technologies to explore, especially in the digital sphere. Many have used the Internet, including social media, to gather data and images for their work. Some create generative art, which use computer programs to set algorithms or rules by which certain images are selected or manipulated. With the rise of AI (Artificial Intelligence), this field is expanding rapidly, introducing questions about whether AI can really create art.

PixCell-Deer#24
Kohei Nawa (Japanese), 2011

The artist coined the term *PixCell* to suggest two tiny entities: cells in biology and pixels in digital images. Here, a taxidermied deer is covered with transparent spheres. When you look closely through the spheres, parts of the deer appear magnified, as if through a laboratory microscope or the zoom function on a computer screen. Kohei Nawa invites us to imagine the results when we use science, and especially new computer technology, to alter biology.

Everyone's Moon 2015-11-04 14:22:59
Penelope Umbrico (Canadian), 2015

Umbrico made this work by downloading from the Internet more than a million photographs people around the world took of the moon. She then put these images in a single file and scanned through them to create a high-speed, flickering video that feels almost hypnotic.

The 49 States

Matthew Jensen (American), 2008–2009

This might look like a bunch of roadside snapshots from an average vacation. However, Jensen created these photos on a virtual road trip using the Google Maps Street View function to navigate his way across the "Lower 48" United States and Alaska.

Where's My Water?

Tabor Robak (American), 2015

Tobak used state-of-the-art digital software to produce this hyper-realistic multi-channel video. When it is on exhibition, it plays across 12 large screens, creating an immersive experience. The glossy, brilliant colors and perfect shadows turn animations of pens, pencils, and brushes jostling around in containers into a hypnotic spectacle.

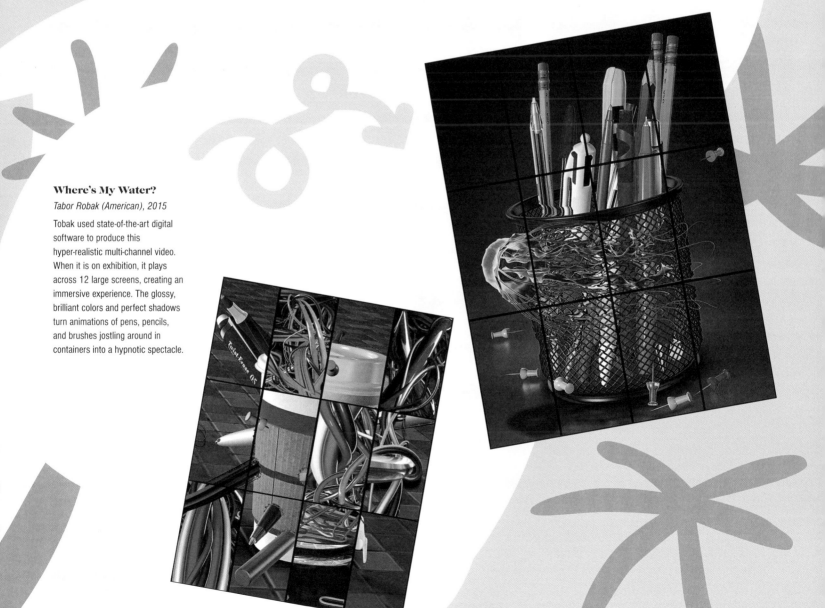

Climate Change

Climate change is one of the biggest challenges facing humans today, as people face extreme weather and fewer natural resources. Many contemporary artists call attention to this crisis in their work, whether through their subject matter or the materials they use.

Untitled (Jardineras)

Damián Ortega (Mexican), 2002

Ortega's work focuses on everyday objects and materials in his native Mexico City. Here, he photographed tiny, rundown garden patches in the city. These examples of neglect emphasize the importance of caring for both the city and its plant life.

Found Art

Some artists worry that art making contributes to the climate crisis. With this in mind, some have embraced using recyclable and renewable materials. The artworks on this page, made from tires, bottle tops, rags, and scrap metal, are excellent examples of innovation meeting sustainability.

Front

Back

Raw Attraction

Chakaia Booker (American), 2001

Chakaia Booker often uses repurposed objects in her work. This piece is made from discarded tires that otherwise would have gone to waste. The artist has cut the tires and arranged them so that they resemble scales or feathers. In this way, human-made, industrial objects now look almost as if they are part of a living creature.

History Refused to Die

Thornton Dial (American), 2004

Dial produced an incredible body of work, assembled from found materials ranging from scrap metal to rags and even the bones of cows he raised. The assorted objects create a gatelike structure, inviting us to reflect on who is kept in or out of spaces and how such experiences are remembered or omitted from history.

Between Earth and Heaven

El Anatsui (Ghanaian), 2006

Anatsui used bottle tops after he found some discarded behind his studio in Nigeria. The caps reflect the waste and environmental damage of consumer culture. By reshaping them and weaving them into his shimmering tapestries, Anatusi continues a practice of West African weaving.

QUIZ
Test your
Knowledge!

Q1

What colored stone is this
water buffalo made from?

Q2

Where is this wall
painting from?

Q3

What metal is
this Chinese
bell made from?

Q5

What was this object
used to burn?

Q4

Where is this feline-
shaped bottle from?

Q6

What kind of instrument is this figure from Cyprus playing?

Q7

Where is this Bodhisattva from?

Q8

What material is this Chinese flask made from?

Q9

This is part of a pack of what?

Q10

What is the shiny coating on this tray called?

Q11
Where does this
print come from?

Q12
What culture is this deity from?

Q13
Where is this
painting from?

Q14
What was the title
given to the king
of Benin?

Q15
Where does
this sculpture
come from?

Q16

Where is this wooden carving from?

Q17

What is this undergarment called?

Q18

Which artist painted this work?

Q20

What discarded rubber objects is this work made from?

Q19

What is the name of this painting by Joan Miró?

Index

49 States, The (Jensen) 241
III (Simpson) 235

A

abstract art 224–225, 228–231
accessories 204–205
Accommodations of Desire, The (Dalí) 227
Acconci, Vito 217
acheiropoieta 106
activism, art and 236–237
Adam and Eve (Dürer) 173
Adoration of the Magi, The (Giotto di Bondone) 165
African art
  Benin bronzes 182–183
  Dogon sculpture 186–187
  sacred stools 188–189
  tracking history 190–191
  Yoruba twin figures 184–185
afterlife 35, 46, 49, 52–53, 76, 78
Afternoon Meal, The (*La Merienda*) (Meléndez) 169
agriculture
  ancient 37
  medieval 129
Akan people 188, 191
Alakzat IV (Bak) 225
Albers, Josef 225
Alexander the Great 54
Allegory of Worldly and Otherworldly Drunkenness (Muhammad) 157
alphabet, Greek 55
altar sets, Chinese 79
altarpieces 128, 164, 170, 171, 183
America Today (Benton) 223
American Revolution 194
amulets 49, 53
Amun 22, 23, 46
Anatsui, El 11, 243
ancestral spirits 183, 187, 188, 198

animals
  in Asian art 74–75, 122
  Chinese zodiac 150, 151
  in Egyptian art 42–43
  Inca 162–163
  materials from 18–19
  medieval bestiaries 129
  symbolism 37
ankh symbol 43
Annunciation, The (David) 171
Annunciation, The (Memling) 171
Annunciation Triptych (Merode Altarpiece) 128
Aphrodite 56, 58
Apollo 58, 59
apprentices 135
aquamaniles 136
Arad, Ron 233
architecture
  Mughal 154
  Timurid 153
Ariadne (Chirico) 222
Arikha, Avigdor 217
Arjuna Battles Raja Tamradhvaja 155
arms and armor 68–73, 193
Artemis 58, 59
Artificial Intelligence 240
Ascent of Mont Blanc, The (Bisson) 211
Asian art
  ancient 74–83
  Buddhism in the Himalayas 124–125
  ceremonies and rituals in China 78–79
  early Buddhist 80–81
  early modern 142–151
  jade in China 76–77
  Japanese fashion and style 148–149
  lacquer 144–145
  landscapes of East Asia 142–143
  medieval 118–127
  porcelain 126–127
  protective deities and guardians 122–123
  silk and paper 120–121

trade 118–119
  zodiac figures 150–151
Assyria 33, 34, 35, 36, 40–41
astronomy 101
Athens 55, 57
Atkins, Anna 211
Attorney Street (Wong) 236
Augustus, Emperor 51, 60, 61, 63
Autumn Rhythm (Number 30) (Pollock) 228
Azhar, Maulana 153
Aztecs 160–161

B

Babylon/Babylonia 33, 34, 35
Bacon, Francis 217
Bak, Imre 225
ball games, Mesoamerican 91
Bandit 201 (Watts) 234
Barbarians, The (Ernst) 226
Bauer, Johann Michael 199
Bazalgette, Joseph 212
Bearden, Romare 230
Beaux, Cecilia 195
Belgium 170–171
Bell, Vanessa Stephen 220
Belles Heures of Jean de France, Duc de Berry, The 132
bells 78, 113
Belter, John Henry 200, 232
Benin Kingdom 182–183
Benton, Thomas Hart 223
bestiaries 129
Between Earth and Heaven (Anatsui) 243
Bi 77
Bierstadt, Albert 210
Bingham, George Caleb 194
Bird in Space (Brancusi) 218
Bisson, Auguste-Rosalie 211
Blake, William 174
Blind Man's Meal, The (Picasso) 221
Block, The (Bearden) 230
Blue Period (Picasso) 221
Blueprint for a Temple

(Woodman) 239
Boccioni, Umberto 222
Bodhisattvas 82, 83, 125
body armor 70–71
bone 19
Book of the Dead 30–31, 53
book painting 155
bookbinding 133, 157
Booker, Chakaia 243
Books of Hours 132
books, printing 173
Boscoreale Roman villa 26, 64–65
Boulevard Montmartre on a Winter Morning, The (Pissarro) 212
Bouquet of Violets, The (Gonzalès) 215
Bousch, Valentin 199
Bowling, Frank 239
Brancusi, Constantin 218
Braque, Georges 219, 232
brass 182
Breton, André 227
Britain 174–175
bronze 23, 78, 79, 182–183
Bronze Age 22
Bronzino 167
Brunel, Isambard 212
Brunel, Marc 212
brushes, paint 120
Buddhism
  across Asia 82–83
  early Buddhist art 80–81
  gold leaf 164
  in the Himalayas 124–125
  medieval art 121, 122–123
  spread of 118
  zodiac figures 150, 151
Buffaloes in Combat (Miskin) 155
Burne-Jones, Edward 174
Byzantine Empire 104–111, 119
  icons 104–105
  luxury goods 110–111, 207
  mosaics 106–107

C

Cadavre exquis (Breton) 227
Caesar, Julius 60, 61
calligraphy
   illuminated manuscripts
   132–133, 164
   Islamic 94, 98–99, 164,
   228
   Mughal 155
Cambodia 75, 122
cameos 63
cames 131
canopic jars 52
*Captain George K.H.
   Coussmaker* (Reynolds)
   175
Caracalla, Emperor 61
Caravaggio 167
Carousel State (Gilliam) 228
carpets 156, 159
Carrington, Leonora 226
cartoons, tapestry 134, 135
carving
   gems 63
   jade 76–77
   stone 16–17, 40–41, 83,
   105
Casey, Samuel 180, 181
Cassatt, Mary 215
Castellani, Firm of 206
casting 23, 38, 79
cathedrals 129, 130
Cathedrals of Broadway, The
   (Stettheimer) 221
Catholic Church 128
cave paintings 14–15, 26
Central and Southern
   America 84–91
   Aztecs 160–161
   Inca 162–163
   Mesoamerican cities
   90–91
   Mesoamerican sculpture
   86–87
   Peruvian art 88–89
ceramics *see* pottery
ceremonial objects 78
Cézanne, Paul 210
Chagall, Marc 223
chain mail 70

chairs 199, 232–233
Champion Single Sculls, The
   (Eakins) 215
Chardin, Jean Siméon 177
Charlesworth, Sarah 233
charms, Egyptian 47
Chavin 85
chess 70
Chess Players, The (Eakins)
   194
China
   ancient 74, 76–79, 82
   Buddhism in 82
   ceremonies and rituals 22,
   78–79
   jade 16, 76–77
   lacquerware 20, 21, 145
   landscapes 142–143
   medieval 120–121,
   126–127
   pottery 24, 118, 126–127
   silk and paper 120–121
   zodiac figures 150–151
Chirico, Giorgio de 222
chocolate 86
Christianity 66
   Byzantine art 104–109
   Flemish art 170–171
   Italian gold paintings
   164–165
   medieval European art
   128–133
   in Ottoman Empire 159
   Spanish art 168, 169
Christo and Jean-Claude 235
churches
   Byzantine 108, 109
   medieval European
   128–134
Circus Sideshow (Seurat) 214
cities
   Aztec 160
   early 32, 33, 36
   late 19th century 212–213
   Silk Road 118
Claude Lorrain 179
clay 24–25, 126
clay tablets 36
Clemente, Francesco 217
climate change 242–243
clocks 101

cloisonné enamel 107, 119
cloth 28–29
clothing 202–205
   Egyptian 45
   Inca 163
   Japanese 148–149
   Ottoman 159
cochineal 135
coins
   Byzantine 105
   Greek 55
   Roman 61
Cole, Thomas 194
collages 230, 239
color 220–221, 224
color, artists of 236, 237
Composition (Mondrian) 224
Composition (Pilaram) 228
Concord (Newman) 228
Cong 77
Constable, John 174, 175,
   179
Constantine I, Emperor 60,
   66, 105, 109
Constantinople 104, 105,
   106, 107, 109, 110
Copley, John Singleton 194
*Coronation of the Virgin,
   and Saints, The* 128
Corot, Camille 178
Courbet, Gustave 178
cowrie shells 184
Cristofori, Bartolomeo 117
Cubism 218, 219, 220, 230
cuneiform 33, 35, 36
cylinder seals 32

D

Dada movement 222
daggers 72–73
Daguerre, Louis 211
Dalí, Salvador 226, 227
Damascus Room 199
*Dance in a Subterranean
   Roundhouse at Clear Lake,
   United States* (Tavernier)
   197
Daubigny, Charles-François
   179
Daulat 155

Daumier, Honoré 177
David, Gerard 171
David, Jacques-Louis 177
David (Monaco) 165
Dead Sea Scrolls 30, 31
Death of Socrates, The
   (David) 177
Degas, Edgar 215
Delaunay, Sonia 223
Demah Barnes, Prince 194
Dendur, Temple of 51
Dial, Thornton 243
diaspora 238
digital art 240–241
Diller, Burgoyne 225
Dogon people 186–187
domestication 37
Douglas, Aaron 221
Dragon Pine 143
dresses 202–203
drums 112, 113
*Duncan Grant in front of a
   Mirror* (Bell) 220
Dürer, Albrecht 172–173
dyers 135

E

Eakins, Thomas 194, 215
Eberle, Abastenia
   St. Leger 197
Edo people 182–183, 191,
   206
egg tempera 27
Egyptians, ancient 42–53
   architecture 50–51
   art for the afterlife 52–53
   gods and goddesses 46–47
   life on the Nile 44–45
   making art 48–49
   materials 16, 17, 18, 19,
   20, 21, 22, 23, 24, 26, 27,
   28
   papyrus 30, 31
El Greco 168, 169
enamel 104, 107, 108, 110,
   119, 133
encaustic paint 27, 67
enlightenment 82, 83, 124
enslavement 238, 239

ere ibeji twin figures 184–185

Ernesta (Child with Nurse) (Beaux) 195

Ernst, Max 226

etchings 172–173

Europe, medieval 128–139
 illuminated manuscripts 132–133
 playing cards 138–139
 stained glass 130–131
 tableware 136–137
 tapestries 134–135

Everyone's Moon (Umbrico) 240

experimental art 234–235

Expressionists 220

F

factories 212, 213

faience 49

fashion 148–149, 202–205

Fauves 220

Fayum portraits 27, 67

featherworks 163

feminism 234

Ferrari, Lorenzo de 201

fertility symbols 186

Fieschi Morgan Staurotheke, The 104

Filipinos Cutting Lettuce, Salinas, California (Lange) 231

Fini, Leonor 227

First Nakamura Tomijuro as a Woman, The (Shunkō) 149

Flanders 170–171

floral style 158

Florence 166

flutes 114, 115

food, for afterlife 52, 53

form 218–219, 224, 228–229

Fortune-Teller, The (La Tour) 176

Fortuny, Mariano 202

Fosso, Samuel 217

found art 243

Four Heavenly Kings 122

Four Horsemen, from The Apocalypse, The (Dürer) 173

Four Hundred Years of Free Labor (Minter) 238

Fragonard, Jean-Honoré 176

France 176–179

Frankenthaler, Helen 225, 229

French Revolution 177

frescoes 26–27, 55, 64–65

Freud, Sigmund 226

funerary objects 37, 52, 89

Fur Traders Descending the Missouri (Bingham) 194

furniture 39, 198–201, 232–233

Futurists 222

G

Gainsborough, Thomas 175

Gamelan 112

Garden Chair, A (Braque) 232

geometric design, Islamic 95, 100

George Washington (Stuart) 194

Germany 172–173

gilders 133

Gilgamesh, Epic of 36

Gilliam, Sam 228

Giotto di Bondone 165

Girl Skating (Eberle) 197

Girls Gathering Shells on the Sea-shore (Utamaro) 147

gladiators 61

Glasgow School 174

glass 45, 63, 130, 180–181

gods and goddesses
 Asian 82, 122–123
 Aztec 160–161
 Chinese 78
 Egyptian 42, 43, 46–47
 Greek 58
 Inca 162, 163
 Mesoamerican 86–87, 160–161
 Roman 66–67
 Yoruba 184

Godwin, Edward William 201

Goes, Hugo van der 171

gold 23, 110

gold leaf 104, 106, 108, 133, 157, 164

Gonchorova, Natalia 219

gongbi 142

Gonzalès, Eve 215

gosho-mage 149

Gospel of St. John 31

Gothic style 128

Goya, Francisco de 168

greaves 70, 71

Greeks, ancient 54–59
 influence of 166
 making art 56–57
 materials 16, 17, 28, 29, 31
 pottery 24, 54, 56, 57, 59, 180
 storytelling 58–59

Grien, Hans Baldung 173

guardian figures 122–123

Guere people 233

Guggenheim, Peggy 229

guilds 135

guitars 116, 117

guns 73

Guo Xi 142

Gutenberg, Johannes 173

H

Hagar in the Wilderness (Corot) 178

Hagia Sophia (Istanbul) 105, 109

Hannart, Johannes 199

happenings 234

Haring, Keith 236

Harlem Renaissance 221

harps 116

Hatch, Alfrederic Smith 197

Hatch Family, The (Johnson) 197

hats 204, 205

Haussmann, Georges-Eugène 212

heart scarabs 53

Heavy Cloud (Kiefer) 238

helmets 68–69, 99

Hemba people 189

Henry VIII of England 70, 71

Hepworth, Barbara 229

Herculaneum 64

Herrera, Carmen 229

Herter Brothers 201

hieroglyphics 42

Himalayas, Buddhism in the 124–125

Hinduism 122

history
 art and 238–239
 visual 191

History Refused to Die (Dial) 243

HIV-AIDS epidemic 236

Höch, Hannah 222

Hofmann, Hans 225

Hokusai, Katsushika 146–147, 213

Holy Family with Saint Elizabeth, Saint John, and a Dove, The (Rubens) 170

Holy Family with Saints Anne and Catherine of Alexandria, The (Ribera) 168

Homage to the Square: On Near Sky (Albers) 225

Homer 31, 58

Homer, Winslow 197

Hopper, Edward 221

horn 19

Horus 46, 47, 51

Hudson River School 194

Hugo, Valentine 227

Humanism 166

I

Iberic (Herrera) 229

Iconoclasm 107, 109

icons, Byzantine 106–107

Iliad (Homer) 58, 59

illuminated manuscripts 132–133, 164

Ilori, Yinka 233

Impressionism 210, 214, 215

Improvisation 27 (Garden of Love II) (Kandinsky) 220

Inca 162–163

India
 ancient 17, 20, 74, 75, 80
 Buddhism 124
 jewelry 206, 207
 Mughal Dynasty 154–155

Indonesia 80, 83, 123

Indus Valley 28, 32, 74

Industrial Revolution 174

industrialization 212

ink 120, 132, 142

Inner Edge (Frankenthaler) 225

insignia 159

installations 238, 239

Intercession of Christ and the Virgin, The 128

Internet art 241

Iran 19, 22, 25, 37, 156–157

Iraq 16, 17, 18, 32–35, 36, 37, 38, 39, 40, 41

iron 23

Ishtar Gate 35
Isis 47, 51
Islamic art
  art of science 100–101
  calligraphy 98–99, 164
  Islamic art 94–95
  mosques 96–97, 198
  Mughal Dynasty 154–155
  Ottoman Empire 158–159
  Safavid Dynasty 156–157
  tiles 102–103
  Timurid Empire 152–153
Italy
  gold paintings 164–165
  Renaissance 166–167
ivory 18, 19, 38, 39, 110

J

Jack of Diamonds Group 219
jade 16, 76–77
Japan
  ancient 19, 24, 25
  Buddhism 83
  fashion and style 148–149
  lacquerware 144, 145
  landscapes 142
  medieval art 121, 122–123
  woodblock prints 146–147
  zodiac figures 150–151
Jeanne Hébuterne
  (Modigliani) 219
Jensen, Matthew 241
jewelry 206–207
  ancient Near East 38–39
  Byzantine 110–111
  Oceania 201
  Roman 62, 63
Joubert, Gilles 200
Juan de Pareja (Velázquez)
  168
Justinian I, Emperor 105,
  108
Justinian II, Emperor 105

K

kaftans 159
Kanbun bijin 149
Kandinsky, Vasily 220
kapkap 193
Kaprow, Allan 234
Kass, Deborah 216
Kastom 192
Kentridge, William 239
keyboard instruments 117

Kiefer, Anselm 238
kilns 25
kimonos 148–149
kings
  Benin 182–183
  sacred stools 188–189
Klee, Paul 225
knights 129
Kollwitz, Käthe 216
Koran 94, 96, 97, 98, 99,
  152, 198
Korea
  ancient 75, 82
  lacquerware 144, 145
  landscapes 143
  medieval 121, 123
Korin, Ogata 146
kosodes 148–149
Krasner, Lee 217
Kruger, Barbara 235
Kufic script 98, 99
Kuniyoshi, Utagama 147

L

La Tour, Georges de 176
La Venta 84, 90
lacquer 144–145
Lady Lilith (Rossetti) 175
Lake of Zug, The (Turner)
  174
Landscape with a Double
  Spruce (Dürer) 172
Landscape with a Sunlit
  Stream (Daubigny) 179
landscapes
  American 196–197
  British 174–175
  East Asian 142–143
  French 178–179
Lange, Dorothea 231
lapis lazuli 16, 37, 38, 98
Last Supper, The (Ugolino da
  Siena) 164–165
leisure time 214–215
Leonardo da Vinci 172
Let My People Go (Douglas)
  221
Lette Eisenhower Ascending
  Ladder in "The Courtyard",
  a Happening (Kaprow) 234
Leutze, Emanuel 194
LGBTQ+ community 236
Limbourg Brothers 132
linen 28, 45
linguists 191

Lippi, Fra Filippo 167
Livia, Empress 61
Locke, Hew 239
London 212
lost wax method 38
Love Song, The (Burne-
  Jones) 174
Lovers among Lilacs
  (Chagall) 223
Luba people 189, 190, 191
Luddites 213
lutes 116
Lydia Crocheting in the
  Garden at Marly (Cassatt)
  215

M

Maar, Dora 226
madder 26, 135
madrasas 97
Majas on a Balcony (Goya)
  168
Mali 186–187
mandalas 124
Mandylion 106
Mangbetu people 191
Mantiq al-tayr 157
manuscripts, illuminated
  132–133, 164
marble 16
Mars and Venus United by
  Love (Veronese) 166
Martini, Francesco di Giorgio
  199
Maso di Banco 165
master craftsmen 135
Matisse, Henri 220
matrilineal societies 189
May Picture (Klee) 225
Maya 16, 21, 84, 86–87, 90
Mecca (Hofmann) 225
mechanization 213
medicine 101
Melancolia I (Dürer) 173
Meléndez, Luis 169
Memling, Hans 171
Memmi, Lippo 164
memory
  art and 238–239
  painting memories 223
memory boards 190, 191
Mesoamerica 16, 20, 21, 22,
  25, 26, 29
  Aztecs 160–161
  cities 90–91

sculpture 86–87
Mesopotamia, ancient 25,
  32–41
Met Cloisters, The 139
metal 22–23, 68–73
Mexico 84, 160–161
Mezzetin (Watteau) 177
migration 239
mihrabs 95, 96, 198
Millais, John-Everett 174
minarets 96
minbars 96, 97
miniatures 154, 156
Minoan civilization 54, 55
Minter, Joe 238
Miró, Joan 226, 227
Miskin 155
Moche 85
models 44, 53, 84
Modigliani, Amedeo 219
Monaco, Lorenzo 165
monasteries 124, 129, 132
Mondrian, Piet 224
Monet, Claude 179, 210
Mongols 94, 119
Monk Nichiren Calming the
  Stormy Sea (Kuniyoshi) 147
Morning on the Seine near
  Giverny (Monet) 210
mosaics 64–65, 108–109
Mosca, Simone 199
mosques 96–97, 109, 153,
  198
Moulin Rouge: La Goulue
  (Toulouse-Lautrec) 214
movement, sense of 167
Mr. and Mrs. I.N. Phelps
  Stokes (Sargent) 195
Mrs. John Winthrop (Copley)
  194
Mrs. N's Palace (Nevelson)
  231
Mughal Dynasty 152, 154–
  155, 156
Muhammad, Sultan 157
mummification 52
Murillo, Bartolomé Estebán
  169
musical instruments 112–
  117
Musicians, The (Caravaggio)
  167
Mycenaean civilization 54

N

Nazca 85, 88
Naskh script 98
Nativity, The (van der Weyden) 170
nature 210–211
Nawa, Kohei 240
Nayarit 25, 84, 86
Near East, ancient 32–41
Neoclassicism 177
Nepal, Buddhist art 125
Netherlands 170, 179
Nevelson, Louise 229, 231
New York City 214, 228, 229
Newman, Barnett 228
Nigeria 182–185
Night Journey (Bowling) 239
nightlife 214–215
Nile Valley 42, 44–45
Nimrud 33, 34, 39, 40
Nineveh 33, 34, 35
Nizami of Ganja 153
Nkisi N'Kondi 190
No. 13 (White, Red on Yellow) (Rothko) 225
nobility 129
Noboto at Shimōsa (Hokusai) 147
Noni people 189
North American art
American portraiture 194–195
American scenes 196–197

O

Oceania 192–193
Odyssey (Homer) 31, 58
Oeben, Jean-François 201
oil paints 170, 171
Old Man and His Young Wife Before Religious Arbitrators, An (Daulat) 155
Old Trees, Level Distance (Gui Xi) 142
Olmecs 84, 86, 90, 91
oral tradition 190
Orchid Pavilion Gathering: Autumn Harvest Festival (Taiga) 142
Ortega, Damian 242
ostraka 48
Ottoman Empire 107, 109, 118, 156, 158–159
outside, painting 179, 210

Oval Form with Strings and Color (Hepworth) 229

P

paint 26–27
paintings
American 194–197
British 174–175
Chinese silk 120
Egyptian 48
Flemish 170–171
French 176–179
Impressionist 210, 214
Italian gold 164–165
Italian Renaissance 166–167
landscapes of East Asia 142–143
modern 220–229, 238–239
Safavid 156
Spanish 168–169
Surrealist 226–227
Pakistan 80, 81
paper 30–31, 98, 99, 120–121
Papua New Guinea 192
papyrus 30, 31
Paracas 25, 85, 88
parchment 30, 98, 99, 132
Paris 194, 212, 214–215
Parsons, Betty 229
Pastoral Landscape: The Roman Campagna (Claude Lorrain) 179
patrons 128, 129
percussion 112–113
Père Ubu (Maar) 226
performance art 234
performing arts 215, 219
Persian Empire 154, 156–157
Peru 85, 88–89
pharmacies 136, 137
photography 210, 211, 220, 231
pianoforte 117
Picasso, Pablo 217, 219, 220, 221
pictographs 36
piece-mold casting 79
Pilaram, Faramarz 228
pilgrims 129
Pindell, Howardena 217
Pintura Constructiva (Torres-Garcia) 225

Pippin, Horace 217, 233
Pissarro, Camille 212
pitchers 136
PixCell-Deer#24 (Nawa) 240
playing cards 138–139
politics 235
Pollock, Jackson 228
Pompeii 64
Pop Art 230
porcelain 118, 126–127
portrait heads 60–61
Portrait of a Man (van der Goes) 171
portrait paintings 174, 178, 194–195, 216–217
Portrait of a Woman with a Man at a Casement (Lippi) 167
Portrait of a Young Man (Bronzino) 167
Poseidon 58
Post-Impressionism 214
Potato (Miró) 227
pottery 24–25
Greek 54, 56, 57, 59
Inca 162
Islamic 101, 102–103, 153
Peruvian 89
vessels 180–181
Poussin, Nicolas 177
Praxiteles 56
Pre-Raphaelite Brotherhood 174
precious stones 63
printing 172–173, 213
private objects 186–187
proportion 173
Prose on the Trans-Siberian Railway and of the Little Jehanne of France by Blaise Cendrars (Delaunay) 223
pyramids, Mesoamerican 84, 87, 90

Q

quill pens 133

R

Raphael 172
rattles 112, 113
Rauschenberg, Robert 231
Raw Attraction (Booker) 243
record keeping objects 190
recyclable/renewable

materials 243
Red Roses Sonata (Thomas) 229
Reformation, Protestant 172
Refusal of Time, The (Kentridge) 239
Rehearsal of the Ballet Onstage, The (Degas) 215
reliefs, stone 40–41, 66–67, 86, 87
religious objects 37, 108
reliquaries 80, 111, 129
Renaissance, Italian 166–167, 169, 177
Repast of the Lion, The (Rousseau) 223
Reynolds, Joshua 175
Ribera, Jusepe de 168
Rietveld, Gerrit 233
Ringgold, Faith 237
ritual objects 37, 77
Robak, Tabor 241
Rocky Mountains, Lander's Peak, The (Bierstadt) 210
Roentgen, David 201
Romanesque architecture 128, 129
Romans 60–67, 109
homes 64–65
influence of 166
making art 62–63
materials 16, 17, 18, 26, 27
religious beliefs 66–67
Rome 166, 178
Rosler, Martha 234
Rossetti, Dante Gabriel 174, 175
Rothko, Mark 225
Rough Waters (Korin) 146
Rousseau, Henri 223
Roux, Alexander 232
Royal Academy of Painting and Sculpture 176
Rubens, Peter Paul 170
rubricators 133
Ruhlmann, Emile-Jacques 201

S

sacred stools 188–189
Safavid Dynasty 156–157
Saint Anthony of Padua (Maso di Banco) 165
Saint Paul (Memmi) 164
Saints Peter and John

Healing the Lame Man (Poussin) 177
Salisbury Cathedral from the Bishop's Grounds (Constable) 175
Samad, Abdus 154
Samarqand 152
Samurai warriors 68
Sargent, John Singer 195
Sayyid Ali, Mir 154
saz style 158
Schiaparelli, Elsa 203, 207, 227
science
  Islamic Golden Age 100–101
  Timurid Empire 152
scribes 36, 44, 132–133
scrolls 30–31, 121, 142
sculpture
  American 197
  ancient Greek 56, 58, 59
  Aztec 160–161
  Benin bronze 182–183
  Buddhist 80
  Dogon 186–187
  early 14, 15
  Inca 163
  Islamic 94–95
  medieval Asian 122–123
  Mesoamerica 86–87, 90–91, 160–161
  modern 218, 229, 231, 239
  Oceania 192
  Roman 60–61, 62, 67
  Yoruba 184–185
  zodiac figures 150–151
Second Theme (Diller) 225
secular subjects 166
Self-Portrait (Carrington) 226
Self-Portrait (Van Dyck) 171
self-portraits 216–217
Semiotics of the Kitchen (Rosler) 234
Serrurier-Bovy, Gustave 201
Seurat, Georges 214
shabtis 49
Shah Jahan on Horseback 155
Shaikh Mahneh and the Villager 156
Shaikh San'an Beneath the Window of the Christian Maiden 157
Shaker style 201

Shang dynasty 78
Shao Fan 233
shells 19
  inlaid 144, 193
Shi'a Islam 156, 228
shields 72–73
Shinto 123
shoes 204
shrines 187
shui-mo 142
Shunkō, Katsukawa 149
Shustak, Lawrence N. 234
silk 28, 118, 120, 148, 156
Silk Road 81, 118, 152
silver 110
Simpson, Lorna 235
Six Pens 98
smalti-tesserae 108
smelting 23
Smith, Art 207
Soap Bubbles (Chardin) 177
Solomon Islands 192, 193
Songye people 189
South America *see* Central and Southern America
Spain 168–169
spinning 28, 29
Spiraea aruncus (Atkins) 211
Spy Hamzar Brings Mahiya to the City of Tawariq, The 10
Sri Lanka 81, 82
stained glass 130–131
statues *see* sculpture
Stazio, Abbondino 199
stelae 16, 17, 47, 53, 56
Stettheimer, Florine 221
Still Life with a Ginger Jar and Eggplants (Cézanne) 210
still lifes 168, 169, 178
Stolen Kiss, The (Fragonard) 176
stone 16–17
stools, sacred 188–189
storage jars 136
storytelling
  Africa 190, 191
  ancient Greeks 58–59
  stone reliefs 40–41
Street Story Quilt (Ringgold) 237
stringed instruments 116–117
Stuart, Gilbert 194
Stubbs, George 175

studiolo (Ducal Palace, Gubbio) 198, 199
stupas 80
suits of armor 70–71
Süleiman the Magnificent, Sultan 159
Sumer 32, 34
Sunni Islam 156
Surrealism 226–227
swords 72–73
Syria, ancient 16, 18, 22, 39, 41

T

Tables for Ladies (Hopper) 221
tableware 75, 79, 129, 136–137, 180–181
Taiga, Ike 142
Tairona culture 207
Take Off (Frankenthaler) 229
Talbot, William Henry Fox 211
tapestries 134–135, 243
tattoos 234
Tavernier, Jules 197
temples 50–51, 58, 59, 160
Teotihuacán 26, 90
terracotta 24, 28, 29, 54, 57, 58, 59, 61
tessellation 100
tesserae 64, 108
textiles 28–29
  Inca 163
  Islamic 100
  Japanese fashion and style 148–149
  medieval European tapestries 134–135
  Ottoman 158–159
  Peruvian 88
  quilts 237
Thailand 74, 83, 122
theater 58, 59, 215, 219
Third Duke of Dorset's Hunter with a Groom and a Dog, The (Stubbs) 175
Third-Class Carriage, The (Daumier) 177
Thomas, Alma 229
Three O'Clock Sitting, The (Matisse) 220
Tibet 124, 125
Tiffany, Louis Comfort 207
tiles 95, 100, 102–103, 153,

159
time 222–223
Timurid Empire 152–153
Titian 167
Tokyo 213
Tolliver, Mose 216
Tomato from Campbell's Soup I (Warhol) 230
tombs 50–51, 52–53, 66
tools, early 14–15
Torres-Garcia, Joaquin 225
Toulouse-Lautrec, Henri de 214
trade
  art and 38
  medieval Asian 118–119
  silk 148
  Silk Road 81, 118
trompe l'oeil 65
tughras 159
Turner, Joseph Mallord William 174, 179
twin figures 184–185

U

uchikakes 149
Ugolino da Siena 164
ukiyo-e 147
Umbrico, Penelope 240
unconscious, the 226
Under the Wave off Kanagawa (Hokusai) 146
undergarments 204, 205
unicorns 135
Unique Forms of Continuity in Space (Boccioni) 222
United States 194–197
Untitled (Jardineras) (Ortega) 242
Untitled (Your Seeing Is Believing) (Kruger) 235
Ur 34
Utamaro, Kitagawa 147

V

Vajrayana Buddhism 124
Van Dyck, Anthony 171
Van Erp, Dirk 201
van Gogh, Vincent 213
Vehicles on the Streets of Tokyo (Yoshitora) 213
Velázquez, Diego 168
vellum 132
Venice 166

Venus and Adonis (Titian) 167

Veronese, Paolo 166

Vietnam 75, 83

View on the Catskill–Early Autumn (Cole) 194

View of Orleans (Courbet) 178

View of Toledo (El Greco) 169

Virgil's Tomb by Moonlight, with Silius Italicus Declaiming (Wright) 175

Virgin and Child (Murillo) 169

Vonnoh, Bessie Potter 197

W

wall paintings 26–27, 48, 105

Warhol, Andy 216, 230

Washington Crossing the Delaware (Leutze) 194

watercolors 142

Watteau, Antoine 177

Watts, Robert 234

weapons 72–73

weaving 28, 29, 88, 134, 135, 243

Wegman, William 233

Weltrevolution (Höch) 222

Weyden, Rogier van der 170

Where's My Water? (Robak) 241

whistles 114, 115

Wild Geese Descending to Sandbar 143

William Duguid (Demah Barnes) 194

wind instruments 114–115

windows, stained glass 130–131

Wine Dark Sea, The (Locke) 239

Wine Drinking in a Spring Garden 153

Winter Pool (Rauschenberg) 231

Winter Trees, Reflected in a Pond (Talbot) 211

Witches, The (Grien) 173

woad 135

Woman in a Chemise in an Armchair (Picasso) 219

women
in American art scene 229
position in society 189

Wong, Martin 236

wood 20–21

woodblock prints 146–147, 213

woodcut prints 172–173

Wooded Upland Landscape (Gainsborough) 175

Woodman, Francesca 239

wool 28, 29

wrapping objects 235

Wright, Joseph 175

writing
early 36
Islamic calligraphy 98–99

X

xieyi 142

Y

Yanagi, Sori 232

Yimam people 200

Yoruba people 184–185

Yoshitora, Utagawa 213

Young Mother, A (Vonnoh) 195

Z

Zeus 58

Zhou dynasty 78, 79

ziggurats 34

zodiac figures 150–151

Answers to Quiz

1
Jade. See page 16

2
Rome. See page 26

3
Bronze. See page 78

4
Peru. See page 89

5
Incense. See page 95

6
An aulos. See page 114

7
Nepal. See page 125

8
Porcelain. See page 126

9
Playing cards. See page 138

10
Lacquer. See page 145

11
Japan. See page 147

12
Aztec. See page 161

13
Spain. See page 169

14
Oba. See page 182

15
The United States. See page 197

16
Papua New Guinea. See page 200

17
Bustle. See page 205

18
Mary Cassatt. See page 215

19
Potato. See page 227

20
Tires. See page 243

Picture credits

The publisher would like to thank the following for their kind permission to reproduce their photographs:

(Key: a-above; b-below/bottom; c-centre; f-far; l-left; r-right; t-top)

11
© El Anatsui. Courtesy of the artist and Jack Shainman Gallery, New York (t).

216
© Estate of Mose Tolliver / DACS 2023 (2).

© Deborah Kass. ARS, NY and DACS, London 2023 (3).

© 2023 The Andy Warhol Foundation for the Visual Arts, Inc. / Licensed by DACS, London (4).

© Estate of Avigdor Arikha. All rights reserved, DACS 2023 (9).

217
Courtesy the artist and Garth Greenan Gallery, New York (7).

© The Estate of Francis Bacon. All rights reserved. DACS 2023 (8).

© Vito Acconci / DACS, London & Artists Rights Society (ARS), New York, courtesy Maria Acconci 2023 (10).

© The Pollock-Krasner Foundation ARS, NY and DACS, London 2023 (11).

© Succession Picasso / DACS, London 2023 (12).

218
© Succession Brancusi - All rights reserved. ADAGP, Paris and DACS, London 2023.

220
© Estate of Vanessa Bell. All rights reserved, DACS 2023 (bl).

221
© Heirs of Aaron Douglas / VAGA at ARS, NY and DACS, London 2023 (tc).

© Heirs of Josephine Hopper / Licensed by Artists Rights Society (ARS) NY / DACS, London 2023 (cr).

© Succession Picasso / DACS, London 2023 (br).

222
© DACS 2023 (tr, cr).

223
© 2023 T.H. and R.P. Benton Trusts / Licensed by Artists Rights Society (ARS), New York & DACS, London (tl).

© ADAGP, Paris and DACS, London 2023 (bl).

225
© DACS 2023 (3).

© The Josef and Anni Albers Foundation / DACS 2023 (4).

© ARS, NY and DACS, London 2023 (5).

© 1998 Kate Rothko Prizel & Christopher Rothko ARS, NY and DACS, London (6).

© Helen Frankenthaler Foundation, Inc. / ARS, NY and DACS, London 2023 (7).

© Estate of Burgoyne Diller / VAGA at ARS, NY and DACS, London 2023 (9).

226
© ADAGP, Paris and DACS, London 2023 (tl, br).

© Estate of Leonora Carrington / ARS, NY and DACS, London 2023 (cra).

227
© Salvador Dalí, Fundació Gala-Salvador Dalí, DACS 2023 (tl).

© Successió Miró / ADAGP, Paris and DACS London 2023 (tr).

© ADAGP, Paris and DACS, London 2023 (crb, bc).

228
© ARS, NY and DACS, London 2023 (br).

© The Barnett Newman Foundation, New York / DACS, London 2023 (cla).

Faramarz Pilaram Foundation (Ali Pilaram) (tr).

© The Pollock-Krasner Foundation ARS, NY and DACS, London 2023 (bl).

229
Barbara Hepworth © Bowness (tr).

© Helen Frankenthaler Foundation, Inc. / ARS, NY and DACS, London 2023 (c).

© 2023 Estate of Alma Thomas / ARS, New York and DACS, London (cb).

© Estate of Carmen Herrera; Courtesy Lisson Gallery (br).

230
© 2023 The Andy Warhol Foundation for the Visual Arts, Inc. / Licensed by DACS, London (t).

230-231
© Romare Bearden Foundation / VAGA at ARS, NY and DACS, London 2023 (b).

231
© ARS, NY and DACS, London 2023 (t).

Library of Congress, Prints & Photographs Division, Farm Security Administration / Office of War Information Black-and-White Negatives (c).

© Robert Rauschenberg Foundation / VAGA at ARS, NY and DACS, London 2023 (crb).

232
© ADAGP, Paris and DACS, London 2023 (br).

233
Ron Arad and Associates (bl).

© The Estate of Sarah Charlesworth. Courtesy Paula Cooper Gallery, New York. Photo: Steven Probert (cb). Sarah Charlesworth, Rietveld Chair, 1981, black and white mural print, mounted with color adhesives in lacquered wood frame, frame: 68 x 50 x 1 5/8 in. (172.7 x 127 x 4.1 cm) AP 2, Edition of 3, + 2 APs.

© DACS 2023 (tc).

© William Wegman, courtesy the artist (cra).

Yinka Ilori MBE; Title: Iya Ati Omo;Artist: Yinka Ilori (British-Nigerian, born London, 1987); Date: 2016; Medium: Beech wood, enamel paint, brass, and cotton; Dimensions: 31 1/4 × 17 11/16 × 18 3/4 in. (79.4 × 44.9 × 50.2 cm); Width with panel open: 25 in. (63.5 cm) (br).

234
© Martha Rosler courtesy of the artist and Mitchell-Innes & Nash, New York.

Title: "Bandit 201". (Stick-on Tattoos for Implosions, Inc.). Offset lithograph, printed on pressure sensitive vinyl with adhesive backing. © Robert Watts Estate, NY. Larry Miller and Sara Seagull. 1967/2023 (b).

Photograph courtesy the Estate of Lawrence N. Shustak (tl).

235
© Christo and Jeanne-Claude Foundation (bl, bc).

© Lorna Simpson. Courtesy the artist and Hauser & Wirth. Photo: James Wang (tl).

236
Copyright Martin Wong Foundation. Courtesy of the Martin Wong Foundation and P·P·O·W, New York (bl).

237
© Faith Ringgold / ARS, NY and DACS, London, Courtesy ACA Galleries, New York 2023 (t).

238
© Anselm Kiefer. Courtesy Gagosian: Anselm Kiefer Heavy Cloud, 1985; Lead and shellac on photograph, mounted on board; 23 3/8 x 34 1/2 in. (59.4 x 87.6 cm) (cl).

© ARS, NY and DACS, London 2023 (br).

239
© Frank Bowling. All Rights Reserved, DACS 2023 (tl).

© Hew Locke. All rights reserved, DACS / Artimage 2022. Photo: Charles Littlewood (cra).

© William Kentridge (br).

© 2023 Woodman Family Foundation / Artists Rights Society (ARS), New York (clb).

240
Kohei Nawa: PixCell-Deer#24; 2011; mixed media; 2020×1820×1500 mm; collection of The Metropolitan Museum of Art, New York, USA; photo: Nobutada OMOTE | Sandwich (cra).

Courtesy Penelope Umbrico and The Met Museum (b).

241
Courtesy of Matthew López-Jensen (c).

Copyright Tabor Robak (bc).

242
© Damián Ortega

243
Courtesy Chakaia Booker and David Nolan Gallery / © Chakaia Booker (b).

© 2023 Estate of Thornton Dial / Artists Rights Society (ARS), New York / DACS, London (tr).

All illustrations © Xuetong Wang

All other images ©MMA

Project Editor Rosie Peet
Editor Rica Dearman
Senior Art Editor Clive Savage
Senior Designers Sunita Gahir, Lisa Sodeau, Michelle Mackintosh
Production Editor Siu Yin Chan
Production Controller Louise Minihane
Senior Acquisitions Editor Katy Flint
Managing Art Editor Vicky Short
Publishing Director Mark Searle

Written by Susie Brooks, Susie Hodge, Dr. Sarah Richter, Mary Richards, and Dr. Aaron Rosen
Illustrations by Xuetong Wang

First American Edition, 2023
Published in the United States by DK Publishing
1745 Broadway, 20th Floor, New York, NY 10019

The Metropolitan
Museum of Art
New York

© 2023 The Metropolitan Museum of Art

Artwork copyright © Xuetong Wang, 2023

Published in Great Britain by Dorling Kindersley Limited

A catalog record for this book
is available from the Library of Congress.
ISBN 978-0-7440-6102-4

DK books are available at special discounts when purchased
in bulk for sales promotions, premiums, fund-raising, or educational use.
For details, contact: DK Publishing Special Markets,
1745 Broadway, 20th Floor, New York, NY 10019
SpecialSales@dk.com

Printed and bound in Slovakia

Acknowledgments
The publisher would like to thank Stephen Mannello, Josh Romm, Rachel High, Leanne Graeff, Jennifer Kelaher, Morgan
Pearce, Liv Stavredes, and Laura Corey at The Met; all the curators from the Egyptian Art, Islamic Art, Asian Art, Greek and
Roman Art, Ancient Near Eastern Art, African Art, Oceanic Art, Ancient American Art, Medieval Art and The Cloisters,
European Paintings, European Sculpture and Decorative Arts, the Costume Institute, Arms and Armor, the American Wing,
Musical Instruments, and Modern and Contemporary departments at The Met; Lisa Silverman Myers; Hilary Becker for
approvals co-ordination and editorial support; Elizabeth Dowsett, Nicole Reynolds, Flo Ward, Victoria Armstrong, and Mary
Richards for editorial support; Kathryn Hill and Heather Wilcox for proofreading; Helen Peters for creating the index; Martin
Copeland, Amy Moss, and Myriam Megharbi for picture research; Xuetong Wang for her illustrations; and Kim Meech.
With special thanks to the authors.

For the curious
www.dk.com
www.metmuseum.org